JANET MELROSE &
SHERYL NORMANDEAU

The Prairie Gardener's Go-To for

Vegetables

T0150859

TOUCHWOOD

Copyright © 2020 by Janet Melrose and Sheryl Normandeau

All rights reserved. No part of this publication may be reproduced, stored in a retrieval system, or transmitted in any form or by any means, electronic, mechanical, photocopying, recording, or otherwise, without the prior written permission of the publisher. For more information, contact the publisher at: touchwoodeditions.com.

The information in this book is true and complete to the best of the authors' knowledge. All recommendations are made without guarantee on the part of the authors or the publisher.

Copy edited by Paula Marchese

Design and Illustration by Tree Abraham

Photos by Janet Melrose and Sheryl Normandeau unless otherwise noted.

LIBRARY AND ARCHIVES CANADA CATALOGUING IN PUBLICATION

Title: The Prairie gardener's go-to for vegetables / Janet Melrose and Sheryl Normandeau.
Names: Melrose, Janet, 1954- author. | Normandeau, Sheryl, author.
Description: Series statement: Guides for the Prairie gardener | Includes index.
Identifiers: Canadiana (print) 20190207248 | Canadiana (ebook) 20190207256 |
ISBN 9781771513128 (softcover) | ISBN 9781771513135 (HTML)
Subjects: LCSH: Vegetable gardening—Prairie Provinces.
Classification: LCC SB323.C3 M45 2020 | DDC 635.09712—dc23

TouchWood Editions gratefully acknowledges that the land on which we live and work is within the traditional territories of the Lkwungen (Esquimalt and Songhees), Malahat, Pacheedaht, Scia'new, T'Sou-ke and W̱SÁNEĆ (Pauquachin, Tsartlip, Tsawout, Tseycum) peoples.

We acknowledge the financial support of the Government of Canada and the Province of British Columbia through the Book Publishing Tax Credit.

This book was produced using FSC®-certified, acid-free papers, processed chlorine free, and printed with soya-based inks.

Printed in China

24 23 22 21 20   1 2 3 4 5

Dedicated to all prairie gardeners

Introduction 6

Introduction

Full disclosure: We are *really* into vegetable gardening! We can't get enough of the thrill of nurturing a tiny seed into a juicy, flavourful tomato, scooped fresh from the plant; questing for potatoes, snugged into hills of warm soil; or grilling up sweet cobs of corn we've grown ourselves at a family barbecue.

We know you feel the same way, and you want your vegetable gardens to be healthy, sustainable, and bountiful. We want to help you work with—not fight—our admittedly interesting climate. We talk a little about botany, so that you can understand how and why specific plants grow the way they do. We also help you troubleshoot when cultural or environmental conditions cause hiccups or wreak havoc with your crops. We often hear the words "challenging" or "daunting" to describe prairie gardening, but our goal is to give you the information and tools you need to soften that term a little and bring it much closer to "rewarding."

As you read this book, you'll find that as we work through the individual answers to your questions, we are also dedicated to helping you become long-term vegetable gardeners, focused on creating healthy gardens that will sustain you, your family, and your community for years to come. We want to encourage you to think about the reasons why it's so important to grow your own vegetables (and other edibles). Producing your own food and bringing it from seed to the table is a powerful way to become more self-reliant and to take back ownership of our sustenance. Food becomes the stuff of life, not just something wrapped in plastic or shoved into boxes on the shelves at the grocery store. We want to emphasize how every living creature works within ecosystems and how we, as gardeners, are responsible for supporting and promoting those life cycles—after all, we are part of them.

From planning to planting, we encourage you to take a fully hands-on approach with your gardens. This includes knowing when—and how!—to transplant your carefully nurtured seedlings in the spring, ways to shelter your plants from that inevitable July hailstorm, and determining how much irrigation is necessary in our arid climate. We're going to help you figure out if you should prune your tomatoes, what types of supports you should use to hold up your pumpkins off

the ground, and how to maximize your harvest by planting in succession. And we're going to show you how you can directly influence the quality of your produce, minimizing problems such as woody radishes, buttoning cauliflower, and split cabbage heads.

Whether you've just acquired your first garden space, or you've been growing vegetables for decades, gardeners are always learning and experimenting, building on experiences and wisdom gained on their own or from others. We want to be a big part of your continuing (ad)ventures and help you achieve success in your prairie gardens! This is not an exhaustive list, but it covers the most common questions that we've been asked over the years. Let's get started!

—SHERYL NORMANDEAU & JANET MELROSE

Define your veggies!

Figuring out what exactly a vegetable is can differ depending on your perspective. Take a look:

Botanically, a vegetable is . . . well, not a fruit. A fruit has an actual scientific definition: It is the fertilized, developed ovary of a seed. (There are a few exceptions, however. Some plants exhibit parthenocarpy, where the fruit matures without fertilization.) A vegetable is pretty much every other part of a plant that is edible, typically categorized by leaves, stems, roots, tubers, bulbs, and—just to make things a bit fuzzy—some flowers (for example, cauliflower and broccoli) and some seeds (like peas).[1]

In common usage, we complicate matters somewhat by calling botanical fruits, such as tomatoes and squash, vegetables. Rhubarb is a prime example of a vegetable categorized as a fruit.

The culinary definition of a vegetable is subjective, based on taste. Generally speaking, if the plant parts are used in savoury dishes, they are usually considered to be vegetables, while plant parts used in sweet dishes are fruits. And then there's the fact that many of us love carrot cake . . .

Grow your greens! (And your reds and purples . . .)

9

Cultivation Practices

1

How much water do vegetables need?

Getting the right amount of water to your plants, when they need it, is essential.

Back in the summer of 2016, many gardeners in Calgary learned a valuable lesson. That summer it rained and rained from June through to the end of August. It was the summer of the monsoon, and gardeners loved it, though sun lovers despaired. For those months, the soil was moist all the way through the soil profile.

What Calgary gardeners learned was how good our edibles looked and tasted with so much water. They were big, succulent, and beautiful.

What we often forget is that edibles, especially vegetables, are mostly water. When we spare the water, they can be tough, thin in texture or woody, bitter, or not have much taste at all. Even more than that, when plants are parched for water, they are stressed, don't grow to their mature sizes, have reduced production, and are prone to disease.

Yet the last thing that we should do is water too much. Waterlogged soil is more detrimental to healthy plants than too little water, and the symptoms of a plant drowning are often similar to the symptoms of too little water. So, the question is always How much is enough?

As always, the answer is in the soil. Before watering, check whether the soil is dry by digging a hole down to where the roots are, typically six inches (fifteen centimetres) deep or more. In a climate of low humidity and windy conditions, the top of the soil will always look dry, so it behooves us to check first.

If you determine that the soil is dry, then go ahead and apply water at the base of the plants, letting it sink in. Watch to see how fast it infiltrates the soil, and if it quickly disappears, then apply more water. We use is the fifteen-second rule. If the water stays on the surface and takes fifteen seconds to penetrate the soil, then you have watered enough. At this point, water will have had a chance to penetrate the soil profile down to where the roots are, which will encourage the roots to go deep. There really isn't a set amount of water that you should apply as weather, soil structure, and texture, plus the demands the plants place on the moisture in the soil, dictate how much is needed.

Allow the soil to mostly dry out before watering again. Should it rain, don't be fooled into thinking the skies have done the job for you. A brief rainfall often just wets the surface. A favourite trick of ours is to go and water (if the soil needs it) after that brief shower or thunderstorm. The water you now apply has an easier time of it and goes right down through the soil profile to those roots.

The result will be plants that aren't "wimps" with shallow roots that need constant attention!

A word to the wise: Do avoid spraying the garden bed with water from a hose, sprinkler, or misting stand. Watering down low gets the water where it belongs faster and there is less wastage. Drip irrigation and soaker hoses are excellent, but do give them time to do their job, then turn them off till needed for another watering.[1] —JM

What are the benefits of crop rotation in the vegetable garden? How should I go about doing it?

Crop rotation is an agricultural practice that can be easily adapted to home gardens with careful planning and record keeping.

The foundation of crop rotation is to avoid successively planting the same edibles in the same spot, season after season, to avoid depleting the soil and to prevent pests building up in the soil. The goals are to improve the health and productivity of your edibles, all the while continuing to improve your soil.

While some nutrients can actively contribute to soil fertility, all plants do not require the same nutrients in the same amounts. Some plants are light feeders, and some place heavy demands on the nutrients in your soil. Plants in the squash and tomato families require more nutrients to produce fruit that we consume; and some members of the Brassicaceae family, such as cauliflower and kohlrabi, also require a considerable amount of nutrients to mature properly. Lettuce, arugula, kale, chard, and many other species grown for their leaves are considered light feeders. Soil-improving crops include peas and beans, which convert atmospheric nitrogen and secrete any excess that they do not require into the soil for other species to use.

Similarly, many of the species common to edible gardens attract specific pests—both insects and pathogens—that overwinter in the soil. Continuously planting the same species in the same location in the garden will provide a ready host for them when the growing season arrives, allowing populations to flourish. Removing their host or most susceptible plants can act to damp down populations and, in some instances, will result in eliminating pests from the garden if they cannot access their specific host. Examples abound, but include insects such as the carrot rust fly (*Chamaepsila rosae*), the Colorado potato beetle (*Leptinotarsa decemlineata*), and the cutworm (*Agrotis*); and pathogens such as the potato late blight fungus (*Phytophthora infestans*), the tobacco mosaic virus (*Tobamovirus*), and the bacterium-like potato scab (*Streptomyces scabies*).

Crop rotation plans are based on providing the maximum time for a crop not to

Eggplant is a member of the Solanaceae family. It should not be planted in the same location year after year.

be repeated in the same area of the garden, to build up the nutrients in the soil, and to deplete populations of pests as much as possible. There are three main systems of crop rotation: rotating between light, medium, and heavy, feeders and soil-improving crops; rotating between roots, leafy edibles, fruit-bearing plants, and legumes; and, finally, by botanical family, which groups plants within their families as most species commonly grown have much the same cultural requirements and are subject to the same pests.

For years I tried to create and follow a crop rotation plan, based on either nutrient requirements or the parts of the plant that would be eaten. It always got too convoluted and was hard to remember, much less follow. On the other hand, rotating by botanical family makes perfect sense to me, plus there is the fun of learning about all the species in each family. Almost a two-for-one win!

The primary vegetable botanical families or genera most gardeners grow on the prairies are: *Allium*, the onion genus; Apiaceae, the carrot family; Asteraceae, which includes lettuce and artichokes; Brassicaceae, the cabbage family; Chenopodiaceae, the beet, chard, and spinach family; Cucurbitaceae, the squash family; Fabaceae, the legume and pea family; and Solanaceae, the tomato and peppers family. Lamiaceae, the mint family that contributes so many of our culinary herbs, can be included in the mix, if desired.

The goal then is to create and implement a plan that rotates each of these families through your garden beds, so that there is a three- to four-year gap before species of a family are planted in the same space again. For example, in the Solanaceae family, there are four main species we grow: tomatoes, potatoes, peppers, and eggplant. All can be grown in the same physical location one year, and you would not plant any of them there the following year, even though potatoes are a root crop and the rest are fruit. All of these edibles have moderate to high nutrient needs, similar cultural needs, such as consistent and ample water and full sun, and are hosts to the same pests. The same would apply to the very diverse Brassicaceae family that encompasses root, stem, leaf, bud, and floret edibles, but all have the same cultural requirements and are subject to the same pests. Growing all your *Brassicas* together allows you to put in place physical barriers against both the flea beetle and the cabbage moth, reducing the ability of those insects to lay eggs on the plants.

Within the macroplan for your rotation, you can select the members of each family to plant in a season, noting whether they are a root, leaf, or fruit edible. You can fine-tune your plan to include not following a root crop with another root in another family. For example, if planting carrots in the Apiaceae family one year, plant leafy spinach in the Chenopodiaceae family the next year instead of beets, which are also a root. You may also choose to include some succession planting with different members of the plant's family to increase productivity.

If your garden has three or more beds, then you can rotate families between the beds with perhaps two to three families within a bed. It gets more difficult if you are limited to a single bed, but one option is to plant a perennial in the middle, perhaps an herb such as tarragon, and rotate the families around it in a wheel of sorts. You can also choose to plant only two to three families per season, which neatly allows for a three-year gap before planting those families again.

Creating a crop rotation plan is an exercise best done in the cold light of winter when we both have the time and are not tempted to go astray and impulsively just tuck something in while planting. Then, armed with a plan, it is easy to make seed purchases and seedlings, which really helps us to stay within budget, too!

Make sure to keep your plan and records up to date, as the key to success is to stick to the plan and fine-tune it each season. Some gardeners stay with paper and pencil, while others have spreadsheets that do the trick. I know of one gardener that uses recipe cards. It doesn't matter what you use, so long as it works for you.

Then, when you just have to have that impulse crop, have a container or two handy so you're ready to plant. I always do![2] —JM

What is succession planting? How does it work?

Succession planting, or successive planting as it is sometimes called, is a technique meant to both increase the productivity of your garden and extend the harvest time for specific edibles.

The central premise is that once a crop is done, you always plant something in its place, which can be very different from the idea that you plant everything all at once, harvest when they are all ready, but don't plant anything more, as it won't mature before the frost kills it.

The easiest way to practise succession planting is to plant a few seeds every couple of weeks, so that the plants mature and can be harvested in waves, rather than all at once. Lettuce is a great example, as we want a summer filled with lettuce for our salads, but if we sow a nice row of, say, twenty seeds, they will all be ready in the same week. Can we eat that much lettuce all at once? But if you sow, say, five to ten seeds to start, then add five more every week, you enjoy a more prolonged harvest, have less waste, plus save your sanity.

The next method involves planting all the crop at once but planting many different varieties that mature at different times. Peas work beautifully sown in this way, as the taller varieties will often take longer to mature. It makes sense as they have more growing to do before they flower and grow pods. Then sow increasingly faster and coincidentally shorter varieties along the rows. All will grow to their proper height and get the sun they need, then you can simply harvest from shortest to tallest plants. Root crops are easily grown in this fashion, but it is not necessary to pay attention to their heights at maturity.

Another variation is to sow different types of edibles that have different germination times, maturity dates, and harvesting techniques, and that can be grown in different physical spaces in the garden. This is a form of intercropping, and a simple example is pairing radishes with carrots. Carrots take up to twenty-one days to germinate and can be a full-season edible, if growing the larger varieties. Radishes, on the other hand, are up by day three or four and are often ready to eat within thirty to forty days. Sowing radishes on either side of a carrot row allows for a quick harvest while the carrots are just getting going, then the space the carrots need to grow is freed up. Growing lettuce with arugula is another example of maximizing your garden space and multiplying your productivity.

Finally, if you are succession planting, when you have finished harvesting the first crop, you can start sowing or planting seedlings of another crop in the same space. An example of this is sowing spinach, either in fall or in early spring as the first crop; then sowing beets; then, as the soil cools in late summer, resowing spinach. This example has the advantage of keeping the crops within one family, Chenopodiaceae, the beet family. Alternatively, the first crop could be radishes, followed by cabbage, broccoli, or cauliflower seedlings, once again staying within one family, Brassicaceae. Once the main harvest has been completed, a cover crop such as fall rye can be sown to improve the soil for next year.

Succession planting, as a technique of intensive gardening, removes nutrients from the soil faster than growing just one crop per season. Do ensure that the soil has plenty of nutrients to start with, then, with each further planting, add fertilizer. You may need to provide additional nutrients as the season progresses, either as a side dressing or with a liquid fertilizer.

Do grow extra seedlings as you sow your garden to have those seedlings handy for transplanting as the season progresses. You will need to ensure that you have enough seed to last the season!

Finally, follow the 80 percent to 20 percent rule. Once you have harvested the main crop, be a bit more ruthless and remove the plants, so that you can get in another crop. That last 20 percent is likely to be less tasty and have fewer nutrients, and there is more than an even chance that either the weather or bugs will get to the crop before you can harvest it.

Viewing your garden space as "real estate" and plotting and planning how you will get the most out of it in a season can be exciting, though it does take more planning and attention to get the results you want. But it is worth it![3] —JM

What types of mulch should I use in the vegetable garden? How much should I apply?

Straw is an effective mulch in the vegetable garden.

Mulch definitely has a place in the vegetable garden and is used to control a number of factors. Mulch can restrict the germination of annual weeds. Covering the soil prevents light from hitting the weed seeds, and, although some will still pop up, your labour to remove them is greatly reduced. With the exception of those made of plastic, mulch also helps minimize moisture loss from the soil and cools soil temperatures, which is a huge deal during our hot, dry summers.

A layer of mulch can serve as protection from soil erosion during heavy rainfalls and high winds. Water will also percolate more slowly down into the soil if there is a mulch covering, which reduces the tendency of the top layer of soil to crust over.

While wood chips are certainly workable with perennial vegetables such as asparagus and rhubarb, something a little more temporary and easily movable is useful for annual veggies. Straw is probably the most popular choice, and if you can get it directly from a farmer, it will be fairly economical. Hay can be used as well, but there tends to be more of a risk of introducing weed seed with hay than with straw. That would definitely be defeating one of the reasons to mulch in the first place!

Grass clippings from your lawn (or your neighbour's) are another option, but they need to be dry, not green. Green clippings will decompose rapidly in the vegetable bed. They will produce high heat and a horrible stench as they break down, neither of which is desirable (and the heat can actually harm plants growing nearby). Also, ensure the grass clippings you use have not been sprayed with any herbicides. They should not contain any weed seeds either.

Mulch should be applied in a two-to-three-inch (five-to-eight-centimetre) layer in the vegetable garden. Do not mound the mulch high up against the leaves and stems of the plants, as that may promote rot.

One detriment to applying mulch in the vegetable garden is that it has the potential to provide a habitat for pest insects or annoying molluscs such as slugs. You may have to weigh the pros and cons of using mulch at some point, but do try using it before making a decision.

Remember, organic mulch, such as straw and grass clippings, will quickly break down and may need topping off every month or so during the growing season.[4] —SN

What is a floating row cover? How do I use it properly?

A floating row cover is literally a gardener's best friend, if you will let it be one!

Manufactured from spunbonded polyester or polypropylene, a floating row cover (FRC) is light as a feather when draped over your garden bed and anchored by mounded soil, stones, or bricks. It will protect your edibles from all sorts of environmental and pest damage. Some gardeners prefer to use white plastic PVC piping to create a hoop and draw a floating row cover over the hoop so that there is greater air circulation and space within. A floating row cover is permeable to rainfall, lets air in, allows light to penetrate yet cuts the intensity of our bright prairie sunlight, keeps humidity within and around growing plants, slows evaporation of soil moisture, and deters pests from laying their eggs. A single layer of FRC can help safeguard plants when the temperatures dip at either end of the season. Thicker weights offer a greater degree of security, but we find that simply doubling or tripling the lightest-weight cover provides ample protection as the nights get colder.

The only downside to using an FRC is the need to hand-pollinate those vegetables that bear fruit and seeds. The white cloth is also a barrier between you and your vegetables, and there is that indefinable sense of loss when you don't see all the lovely foliage of the plants you are growing. But the cons against a floating row cover are outweighed by the benefits, especially when everything is still standing after a sudden hailstorm.

After sowing or transplanting our beds early in the season, we put an FRC overtop to provide that buffer of warmth and to prevent soil from drying out quickly, which creates ideal conditions for both germination and early growth or for seedlings to settle in with little transplant shock. We like to keep the cover on as the plants grow in our highly variable spring conditions and swear that those early greens mature much faster. Leaving an FRC on during the summer heat and storms, not to mention when it's prime insect egg-laying season, means that there is less damage from wind, heavy rain, and dreaded hail, while insects try in vain to get to the cabbages, carrots, and spinach leaves.

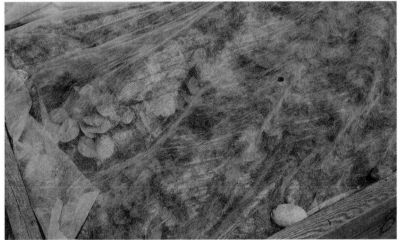

Floating row cover has huge benefits!

During the heat of August, those edibles remain succulent, tasty, and prolific, as they do not suffer sun scorch or excessive moisture loss from drying winds. Then the early fall frosts are flicked off the cover, allowing for an extended harvest.

Proof of the pudding, so to speak, can be seen in October when everything under the floating row cover is still harvestable after a deeper frost, with only those nasturtiums that didn't stay within the protection looking very much the worse for the wear.[5] —JM

When should vegetable seedlings be thinned? How do I go about doing it?

Sometimes it just doesn't matter how steady your hand is or if you use a seeder. Some seeds are astonishingly tiny or oddly shaped, and it can be extremely tricky to space them properly when sowing. Despite your best efforts, you end up dumping a pile of them in the same planting hole. Other times, you generously oversow to guard against poor germination rates.

Overcrowding can be detrimental in the vegetable garden. Plants that are spaced too closely together compete for space, nutrients, water, and light. Air circulation may be restricted. There may be a higher risk of attack from pests and diseases. Yields may be affected.

Your seed packages will tell you the recommended spacing for every type of plant you grow. There is one exception to the guidelines offered: If you are intent on harvesting plants such as leafy greens when they are young and tender, you can group them closer together. If you grow them to maturity, give them the space needed to do so.

Using seed tape instead of individual seed will help eliminate the task of thinning. The seeds in seed tape are already properly spaced, so all you have to do is plant the tape and wait. The tape is biodegradable.

The cotyledons, or seed leaves of a plant, sprout up first, followed by pairs of true leaves. Wait to thin seedlings until the plants have had a chance to produce one or two sets of true leaves. The plants will usually be at least two inches (five centimetres) tall at this point. Lightly dampen the soil before starting to thin the plants—it makes the job easier. For leafy greens, gently pull them up by the roots, being careful not to disturb the surrounding plants. Don't try to thin root crops and plants with large seeds, such as beans and peas. It will cause too much of a disturbance to the soil and the plants growing around them, so use a pair of long-bladed scissors to cut them down at the base of each plant, right near the soil line.

Don't waste the plants you pull! Many thinnings, such as those from kale, spinach, arugula, kohlrabi, and lettuce, can be eaten. Save them, rinse them off thoroughly, and add them to salads and sandwiches. — SN

Give your plants enough space to grow — it boosts the quality of your harvest.

What are the best "bang for your buck" vegetable selections, the ones that produce the most yield per plant?

Many a gardener has limited space to grow edibles. The challenge then is to get the most produce from the plants you grow. Other gardeners love getting lots of harvest from each plant! Either way, some of the best "bang for your buck" vegetables for the prairies are:

* Arugula
* Asian greens—mizuna, mustard, tatsoi
* Cherry tomatoes
* Endive and escarole
* Kale
* Lettuce
* Pole and runner beans
* Potatoes
* Snap and snow peas
* Spinach
* Swiss chard
* Zucchini[6]

Cherry tomato plants are seriously productive!

Weather and Environmental Disorders

2

How do I prevent transplant shock?

Transplant shock is inevitable every time we, as gardeners, take a seedling from where it is currently growing and plant it in another location. It is like giving the plant a root canal. We know how lousy we feel after undergoing such a procedure, so why should it be different for seedlings when their roots have been disturbed in the process of being planted?

The trick is to minimize the shock the seedling undergoes when being planted.

Before even planting, try to buy or grow seedlings that have root systems that are extensive and healthy. Root-bound seedlings are often stressed to begin with and will need to have their roots worked on to loosen them. You may even have to rip some of the dry and matted roots away. As a rule, smaller seedlings are a better bet than larger ones, as they will not have been growing in small cell packs or pots for as long.

Seedlings grown inside your home or in greenhouses need to be gradually acclimatized to the conditions they will be planted in. The process is called "hardening off," which enables the plants to toughen up at the cellular level as they are exposed to increasing amounts of sun, wind, temperature variations, and lower humidity over a period of days. In this process, plants are placed in increasingly harsher conditions around the garden until they have been exposed to and are comfortable with the conditions where they will eventually be. Alternatively, seedlings can be set outside and covered with a floating row cover that is removed for increasingly longer periods of time over a number of days.

Choose your time to transplant well with cooler, overcast days being better than hot and sunny ones. End of day toward dusk is also better than the morning as the newly planted seedlings will benefit from a cooler night to settle in before the sun rises the next day. If you can transplant just before a period of rainy days, that is even better!

Prior to transplanting—a day or so ahead—water both the bed where the seedlings will go and the plants in their containers. Transplanting disturbs the tiny root hairs where most of moisture uptake occurs, so to have the seedlings' roots and leaves fully charged beforehand will minimize the stress they are about to undergo. Soil with good moisture content already will allow for new root hairs to establish quickly.

When removing a plant from its pot, the goal is minimal injury to the root system. We recommend merely loosening the roots and soil so that, once in the soil, the roots will be able to easily grow into the soil of the bed. A good technique is to squeeze the container to loosen the plant inside, and then, placing your hand with fingers widespread under the stem of the plant, turn over the pot, and let the plant fall out of its container. "Tickle" the soil and roots to loosen them before righting the plant and placing it in an already-prepared hole. If an established plant is being divided or relocated, the goal is to take as much of the root ball as possible as the removal of the fine root hairs may cause the plant to have difficulty establishing in its new bed.

Using a product that contains mycorrhizal fungi is often helpful to quickly establish seedlings or relocated plants. The fungi attach to the roots and greatly assist seedlings in the uptake of moisture and nutrients, and help them to develop extensive root systems. Simply sprinkle a little in each hole before planting or have a bowl handy with some in it. Place the seedling in the hole and rub the root ball into the fungi so there is good contact before covering with soil.

If the seedling is in a coconut (coir) fibre or peat pot, or even a newspaper pot, and you want to plant it—pot and all—do slash or tear the sides and bottom of the pot, so that the roots can grow through and access the surrounding soil. Our colder soils really slow down the process of degrading these pots over the course of the season to the point that we often find pots still intact at the end of the season. Make sure that the rim of the pot is below the soil level too.

Once the seedlings are planted, do water them well, but do not flood the soil as that will force air out of the soil pores and may cause the seedlings to drown.

Cover the seedlings with a cloche or a floating row cover for a few days while they establish themselves in their new homes. The extra protection from sun and wind will pay dividends as the seedlings settle in faster and resume growing.

Then be patient. It is natural for those seedlings to be feeling a little the worse for wear after all that they have gone through. But all your care will ensure that they recover quickly and start growing vigorously!—JM

Spinach frequently bolts in hot weather.

Some of my vegetables are going to seed early in the season, before I have a chance to harvest them. Why are they doing this?

This annoying (to us) characteristic is called bolting. It's a survival mechanism, whereby plants pretty much entirely abandon making leaves and instead produce flowers and seed in a huge rush. They do this in response to stresses such as long periods of hot weather (which warms the soil up), drought, lack of nutrients, and changes in day length. Even prolonged chilly temperatures will inspire bolting in certain plants. Cool-weather plants are highly susceptible to bolting—anything in the Brassicaceae family immediately comes to mind, as well as lettuce and spinach. By getting down to making seeds so quickly, the plants are trying to guarantee that there will be another generation after they are dead and gone.

On top of going to seed prematurely, bolting renders plants pretty much inedible. They become tough and woody, and chemical compounds called sesquiterpene lactones make them taste bitter. (Incidentally—and interestingly—these compounds are used by plants as a type of pest resistance.) If you are able to catch plants in the act of bolting and they haven't yet produced seeds, you may still be able to eat the produce. The edible roots of veggies, such as beets and turnips, are usually unaffected by bolting (just the tops are bothered).

There are a number of things you can try to combat bolting, including:

* Plant bolt-resistant cultivars. (That information should be listed on the seed package or in the seed catalogue.)
* Mulch plants and water regularly.
* Use shade cloth around susceptible plants in hot weather.
* Plant cool-weather crops earlier in spring, if possible, so that they are not actively growing in the heat of midsummer. Depending on the weather, you may also be able to start cool-weather crops in late summer for an autumn harvest. The cooler weather will prevent bolting.[1]—SN

Some of my vegetable plants have scabby, ribbed striations or blisters on the leaves—what is this caused by and how can I prevent it?

Oedema is a possibility, particularly if growing conditions have been less than optimal. A combination of high humidity, cool overnight temperatures, and heavy soil moisture over a prolonged period may cause the interior cell walls of plant foliage to swell and rupture. Plants keep trying to take up water through their roots, but they cannot properly transpire (lose) the moisture from the leaves as they would in better circumstances. If you see blisters or leathery blotches on the leaves, and corklike ribbing on the leaf ribs, stems, or petioles of the plants, it's a safe bet that it may be due to oedema. In severe cases, oedema may cause the stems of plants to thin and growth may stop entirely. The fruit of tomatoes or squash may be affected, causing watery blotches on the surface of the skin.

Oedema is common in greenhouse environments, due to the high humidity, but it can also occur in outdoor gardens. Many veggies are susceptible to oedema, including most *Brassicas* (such as Brussels sprouts, broccoli, cabbage, and cauliflower), potatoes, tomatoes, squash, pumpkins, and cucumbers.[2]

Although you cannot control the weather, carefully monitoring how much you water can help. Do not offer a lot of water during times of high humidity.

Good air circulation is also important. Check the seed package recommendations to determine proper spacing. In a greenhouse setting, crank open those vents! If your plants have very dense foliage, it may be useful to prune a few select leaves to open up the crowns a little.[3]

If conditions improve, plants may recover from oedema. A minor case of oedema may cause merely cosmetic damage to plant leaves, so there is no need to remove them. Unfortunately, in the rare cases where the plant stems have shrunk and the uptake of water and nutrients is compromised, there may be no recovery. If the plants are ready to harvest when you discover the problem, fruits affected by oedema may be eaten; you can simply peel or cut the blisters away. If the fruits are not yet mature on the plants, remove them and compost them, as the wounds on the skins may have allowed pests and pathogens inside.—SN

My tomato (or strawberry) fruits are deformed— what could this be from?

"Catfacing" is the term that is applied to fruit that is malformed. Deep cracks may develop, or the skin of fruit may show scar tissue or swelling as it matures. Called catfacing because the deformities sometimes resemble a small cat's face, this is a physiological condition that can occur on many fruits, including apples and pears, but it most often appears on tomatoes.

The disorder is most likely caused by temperatures below 50°F (10°C) being experienced when the fruit is either blossoming or setting after pollination. On the prairies, catfacing is prevalent due to cooler nights and the probability of below 50°F (10°C) occurring at any time. Other potential causes are excessive amounts of nitrogen in the soil and exposure to herbicides, especially 2,4-Dichlorophenoxyacetic acid (2,4-D).

To prevent, or at least limit, catfacing, do choose smaller varieties rather than the very large beefsteak or slicing tomatoes. Buy smaller seedlings in spring and grow them either indoors, in cold frames, or in small greenhouses, rather than trying to grow bigger plants that are already flowering in the greenhouse. Wait to plant them outside well past the danger of cold nights and even light frost. My tomato planting date in Calgary is June 10, as that is the last date we have experienced frost recently. Do protect the plants with a floating row cover for the first few weeks, as the row cover will moderate temperatures at night. A milk jug of water placed by the plants, to absorb heat during the day and to radiate that heat out at night, will also help.

Despite your best efforts, should your tomatoes develop catface, don't compost them. They are perfectly edible and make great salsa or sauce.

As an aside, catfacing in strawberries may also be caused by insects feeding on the flowers or developing fruit. Lygus bugs or tarnished plant bugs (*Lygus* spp.) are often the culprit. The adults overwinter in plant debris, so the best course of action is to clear away dried leaves and other litter around your strawberry plants in the fall.[4] —JM

(TOP) *These onions have been hit hard by hail. They will rebound in time, and the bulbs will not be harmed.* (BOTTOM) *These tomatoes have been pockmarked by hailstones.*

What can I do to fix my vegetable garden after a hailstorm has shredded it? Is there anything I can do to prevent the damage in the first place?

It may be devastating to see your plants suffer such incredible damage, but you'll find that in most cases, vegetables are remarkably resilient. Hailstones and driving wind and rain may cause defoliation, tearing of leaves, and breaking of stems. Flowers and fruits may be bruised or completely knocked off. It can take many weeks for the new leaves and stems to grow back (and, in the meantime, you might weep every time you go into the garden and see the plants in such a condition), but with patience, things will perk up in time. (If your plants are just emerging from the soil and a hailstorm hits, you may not be so lucky. Replanting may be the only recourse.)

It's better not to trim away damaged leaves on most crops—whatever leaf surface is available is still needed for photosynthesis. If only the outer leaves of greens such as lettuce have been pulped, you can cut them away and leave the rest of the plant to grow. Keep the plants as stress-free as possible during their recovery. One of the keys to accomplishing this is to maintain a regular, consistent watering schedule. Monitor your garden for pests and diseases that may take advantage of the opportunity to further weaken injured plants.

If your vegetable beds are hammered by hail on a regular basis, the use of hoop tunnels and high-quality row cover fabric made from polypropylene is a lifesaver. (Don't cheap out and buy low-grade poly—the hailstones will go right through it.) A hoop tunnel covered in aluminum or fibreglass screen will work as well. The benefit of hoop tunnels and row covers is that you can leave them in place all the time, which lessens the panic if you're not home when a storm hits. If you can get outside before the arrival of the storm, you can place heavy glass cloches over individual plants or—in a pinch—overturned buckets anchored to the ground with stakes or weighed down with large rocks.[5] —SN

Frost! It's the bane of the garden in late spring and early autumn. What can I do to protect my plants when the forecast is dipping uncomfortably?

Plants with tender new growth and warm-season crops like tomatoes, squash, and corn are easily damaged by frost. (Root and leafy vegetables are less susceptible, but a hard frost can still cause injury.) Frost causes the water in the cells of plants to expand, then the cell walls will burst. The next day, you'll know something is wrong when stems and leaves are limp and look as if they are water-soaked. As temperatures warm and the plants dry out, the affected tissues may shrivel and blacken.

Carefully watch the forecast during those weeks when frost may be a threat. Clear, calm nights have the most potential for frost, but don't completely discount windy or cloudy conditions. Gather supplies so you can cover plants when the advisories come in; you don't want to be scrambling around in the dark fumbling with blankets and cloches, because when the heat of the day quickly disappears, your plants will be exposed to the chill. Covers can be as simple as old blankets and sheets, or overturned plant pots or buckets. If you are growing plants in containers and they are portable, move them into a garage or other building overnight. You may need to stake or tie down protective covers in case a wind comes up overnight.

Milk jugs are inexpensive, readily available items that work well as cloches.

If it is feasible, setting up a hoop tunnel and employing a high-quality floating row cover fabric or garden fleece can be a huge time saver, eliminating the need to go out every evening and cover individual plants. The fabric must seal the entire structure to keep the radiant heat from the soil trapped inside. Don't forget to open the structure during the daytime. If you choose to cover your plants with blankets or other materials, remove the protection after the frost leaves the ground the next morning.

Frost has damaged these nasturtiums.

Proper siting can help minimize the risk of frost. Frost pockets can happen in low areas at the base of slopes; it is best to locate plants on high ground instead. Plants growing in frost pockets may actually freeze, even if the ambient temperature does not drop below zero degrees. I've had zucchini plants freeze in late August at 39°F (4°C) in a community garden, situated at the bottom of a hill. Slope matters a great deal! —SN

As long as the soil doesn't freeze, potatoes can be harvested late in the season. It's best to get them out earlier, however.

Does frost enhance or sweeten the flavour of some fruits and vegetables? Which ones? How much frost can they take?

Light frost is usually defined as up to 32°F (0°C). Hard frost comes with colder temperatures as there is a greater likelihood that water molecules in plant cells will freeze and then thaw, damaging the cellular walls. This is most evident in edibles that originated in equatorial areas of the world, which do not tolerate chilling temperatures at all and turn to black mush with the lightest of frosts, as they quite rightly have never experienced the cold temperatures that can be found on the prairies!

As fall approaches, many edibles from northern temperate regions have developed mechanisms to withstand colder temperatures. Similar to trees and shrubs preparing to go dormant for winter, species in the cabbage, carrot, and onion families will convert starch molecules to sugar molecules, which do not freeze as readily. Hence the noticeably sweeter taste of carrots, parsnips, beets, chard, leeks, kale, cabbage, Brussels sprouts, cauliflower, turnips, and rutabagas after cooler evenings and light frosts.

A word to the wise, though: Edibles grown for their leaves may become tougher due to cellular changes. No longer palatable in fresh dishes, they are excellent when cooked.

Root crops may be left safely in the soil until needed, so long as the soil does not freeze. Ensure that the soil is moist but not wet, and cover with a floating row cover to protect the foliage from light frosts. Should frosts become heavier, mulch with straw or burlap sacks to prevent repeated freezing/thawing of the upper soil, which can lead to cracking of the flesh of edible fruits and vegetables. This is most often seen in carrots that display lengthwise cracks down the roots. Potatoes left in the ground may also accumulate more scab.[6] —JM

What does herbicide damage commonly look like in tomatoes and other plants? What can I do to help my plants recover?

Evident in this tomato plant, leaves that cup inwards are a sign of herbicide damage.

Herbicide damage can mimic damage caused by other environmental factors, including lack of nutrients, drought, and heat. Plus, we do tend to first think of a biotic cause (living organism) before considering other potential reasons.

As with diagnosing any problem with your vegetable plants, first look at what has happened in the past few weeks in terms of weather, human activity, health of other plants in the garden, and even what is happening to the plants in nearby gardens.

Do learn some of the common symptoms of herbicide damage, so that it forms part of your diagnostic kit, so to speak, as most herbicide damage in home gardens is accidental rather than deliberate, but is always something to think about.

Herbicide damage can occur from soil or water-borne or airborne applications. It can happen through herbicide drift, when someone is applying herbicide as a foliar spray that literally drifts on a breeze and into your garden. It can appear in your soil through leaching from another garden or by bringing in soil or soil amendments that had herbicide applied at some point. Herbicides are often designated as non-systemic, which break down in the soil extremely quickly, or systemic, which can be active in the soil for many years. As a point to note, there is evidence that even non-systemic herbicides are being found in the commercially grown edibles we consume.

Suspect herbicides as the cause if the damage is appearing on more than one plant, if one side of the plant is more affected than the other side, or if damage is more severe in one portion of the garden than the other. But do eliminate other causes before making the determination. Even then, it is a good idea to take a sample of a plant to a local garden centre for confirmation.

Damage can include: distorted growth of stems and petioles; leaves cupping inwards; dwarfing of leaves; discoloured or bleached foliage that turns yellow and then brown; and the plant may stop growing. Depending on the severity, the damaged plants may eventually die.

Tomatoes and others in the Solanaceae family are highly sensitive to exposure to herbicides and are often the ones that are the "canaries" in the garden that initially show harm. As they are large plants, in general, the damage is easy to spot, but do note that if your tomatoes have been exposed to herbicides, then the rest of your garden crops have also been affected.[7] —JM

Mind your soil temperatures! Should we plant on May 24?

The May long weekend has an almost mythological status for prairie gardeners—for many, it represents the magical date when it's safe to plant your garden. In truth, things are not so cut and dried: There are several factors that influence whether or not it's worth it to take a risk to get all that seed into the ground and your lovingly grown transplants out of the house and into the wide world.

It's absurdly obvious, but the weather plays a huge part in our decisions to plant. Possibilities include snow, rain, wind, and blistering heat, sometimes all in the same weekend. Daytime temperatures may be lovely, but the nighttime lows can approach or even plummet below zero. Scrutinize the long-range forecast and plan accordingly. Our season is brutally short, but waiting a week or two to get going won't spell complete disaster when it comes to harvest time for most veggie crops.

Another important thing to remember is to ensure your transplants (or newly purchased plants) are sufficiently hardened off before putting them outside for the rest of the growing season. The hardening-off process can take up to two weeks, if done properly; it involves placing your tender plants in a sheltered location out of the wind and direct, scorching sunlight during the day and returning them indoors overnight. This gives them a chance to slowly acclimatize to the harsh outdoor conditions.

Whether or not your vegetables are cool-season or warm-season matters as well. Cool-season veggies are better equipped to handle the cold, and they may be sown directly or transplanted when the soil and air temperatures are still on the chilly side. Vegetable crops, like all plants, have a higher rate of successful germination within a specific range of temperatures. Although you can definitely sow your seeds when the soil and air temperatures hit the recommended minimums, for best results, aim to plant when the soil and air temperatures reach the optimal range. A soil thermometer may be a useful item in your garden tool kit; you can purchase one at most garden centres or online.

It's best to plant cool-season crops early in the growing season, as the quality of produce may be reduced in hot weather. (If you've ever eaten bitter lettuce or spinach, you'll know what we mean!) Non-resistant varieties may also bolt (flower, then go to seed) in the heat.

As our growing season is so short on the prairies, warm-season crops are often started indoors for transplanting. If you plan to sow warm-season vegetables directly into the garden, wait until after the last frost date in of the spring.[8]

This beautiful Romanesco broccoli is a cool-weather crop.

VEGETABLE CROP	MINIMUM SOIL TEMP. (°F/°C)	MINIMUM AIR TEMP. (°F/°C)	OPTIMUM SOIL TEMP. (°F/°C)	OPTIMUM AIR TEMP. (°F/°C)
Beans	59/15	50/10	73.4–84.2/23–29	60.8–75.2/16–24
Beets	39.2/4	44.6/7	73.4–78.8/23–26	59–64.4/15–18
Bok choi	39.2/4	41/5	64.4–84.2/18–29	59–64.4/15–18
Broccoli	39.2/4	41/5	64.4–84.2/18–29	59–64.4/15–18
Brussels sprouts	39.2/4	41/5	64.4–84.2/18–29	59–64.4/15–18
Cabbage	39.2/4	41/5	64.4–84.2/18–29	59–64.4/15–18
Carrots	39.2/4	44.6/7	73.4–78.8/23–26	59–64.4/15–18
Cauliflower	39.2/4	41/5	64.4–84.2/18–29	59–64.4/15–18
Cucumbers	59/15	60.8/16	69.8–84.2/21–29	64.4–75.2/18–24
Kale	39.2/4	41/5	64.4–84.2/18–29	59–64.4/15–18
Kohlrabi	39.2/4	41/5	64.4–84.2/18–29	59–64.4/15–18
Lettuce	35.6/2	44.6/7	64.4–69.8/18–21	59–64.4/15–18
Onions	32/0	44.6/7	69.8–73.4/21–23	55.4–75.2/13–24
Peas	39.2/4	44.6/7	64.4–69.8/18–21	60.8–64.4/16–18
Peppers	50–59/10–15	64.4/18	73.4–84.2/23–29	69.8–75.2/21–24
Potatoes	44.6/7	44.6/7	60.8–75.2/16–24	60.8–64.4/16–18
Radishes	39.2/4	44.6/7	73.4–78.8/23–26	59–64.4/15–18
Rutabaga	39.2/4	41/5	64.4–84.2/18–29	59–64.4/15–18
Spinach	35.6/2	44.6/7	64.4–69.8/18–21	59–64.4/15–18
Summer squash	59/15	60.8/16	69.8–84.2/21–29	64.4–75.2/18–24
Sweet corn	50/10	50/10	69.8–84.2/21–29	59–75.2/15–24
Swiss chard	35.6/2	44.6/7	64.4–69.8/18–21	59–64.4/15–18
Tomatoes	50–59/10–15	64.4/18	73.4–84.2/23–29	69.8–75.2/21–24
Turnips	39.2/4	41/5	64.4–84.2/18–29	59–64.4/15–18

Using soil and air temperatures as a guideline can take some of the guesswork out of the question "To plant or not to plant?"[9]

Garlic, Onions, and Leeks

3

When is the best time to plant garlic? What are some tips and tricks for best results?

This garlic was planted the previous autumn and is growing nicely.

Garlic, specifically hardneck garlic, is best planted in the autumn months in order for it to establish roots before the prairies freeze up. It is always difficult to specify an exact time for planting, given the widely variable weather on the prairies during these months, but the safe bet is after the autumnal equinox when the soil temperatures are cooling off. The cloves will grow roots but won't sprout. Should the weather become unseasonably warm after you have planted and the garlic sprouts a bit, there is no cause for alarm. Simply mulch the garlic to protect the soil and the cloves nestled below from freeze/thaw cycles over the winter. Leaves, straw, or even old burlap sacks will do the job nicely.

It pays to select your garlic carefully, with hardneck varieties in the Porcelain, Rocambole, or Purple Stripe groups being best for prairie conditions. But it is always worth planting other varieties to see how they grow in your garden.

Garlic prefers weed-free, friable, well-draining soil with a pH range of 6.0–7.5 and excellent fertility. Before planting, amend your soil with compost to improve soil workability and buffer the pH, especially in alkaline soils. Take the opportunity to mix in a fertilizer with a good balance of nitrogen, phosphorus, potassium, and sulphur.

Garlic should be planted six inches (fifteen centimetres) apart as the plants do need space to develop good-sized bulbs and at least four inches (ten centimetres) deep so that the tip of the clove is no less than two inches (five centimetres) below the surface of the soil.

Once spring arrives, pull back any mulch to allow the soil to warm up faster. Once the garlic is sprouting, mulch can be reapplied carefully to conserve moisture and deter weeds.[1] —JM

When do I harvest scapes from hardneck garlic?

Scapes are the flowering stalks of garlic plants. Scapes will eventually produce small white flowers, followed by seeds called bulbils. If you're not growing garlic for seed, it is advisable to remove the long, curly scapes before they bloom. (This way energy will be diverted to producing plump bulbs underground.) Just trim the scapes to the first set of leaves using a pair of sharp, long-bladed scissors. The great thing about scapes is that they are edible! They impart a mild, sweet garlic flavour to stews, soups, stir-fries, and egg dishes. —SN

Hardneck garlic produces delicious scapes.

Should I plant garlic and potatoes purchased from the grocery store?

The main reason why it is not the best idea to plant either garlic or potatoes (or even sweet potatoes) from the grocery store is because they may be sprayed with anti-sprouting chemicals. Some will sprout, albeit slowly, and grow weakly.

Additionally, as they are grown through cloning, pathogens may have accumulated in their flesh that don't affect us when eaten but may appear when planted and spread, causing widespread damage. A noteworthy instance is the Great Famine of 1845 in Ireland. The main potato variety, 'Lumper', widely grown in Ireland at the time, had no resistance to the introduction of a late blight (*Phytophthora infestans*) strain; the resulting famine killed about a million people. As grocery stores source their produce globally, there is a danger of introducing a pathogen that varieties grown in Canada will not have genetic resistance to.

Certified seed potatoes that have been tested to ensure they do not carry disease are a better option and not much more expensive. A bonus is that you are able to select from many varieties bred for particular qualities such as: early-, mid-, or late-season maturity; use in the kitchen, from baking to boiling to roasting; size, from fingerlings to large baking potatoes; and many different shapes and taste profiles. Compared to the choice of yellow, white, or red potatoes common in grocery stores, why not grow something special in your garden?

Garlic is not generally sold as certified stock in Canada; however, the same criteria apply regarding the sources, quality, and varieties of garlic for sale for consumption rather than planting. Garlic growers tend to keep the best of the crop to replant themselves or to sell as seed garlic! That said, lately there are more hardneck varieties available online, at farmers' markets, in organic food and mainstream stores, and from garlic exchanges that are entirely worthy of being grown in your garden. Our golden rule is that it is imperative that we know and trust the source of our garlic stock. — JM

Onion sets versus onion seeds: What are the pros and cons of growing each?

First, let's pinpoint what exactly an onion "set" is. These are onions that were planted from seed the year before and harvested before they were fully mature. They were then carefully stored and marketed to gardeners the following spring. The reason onion sets are popular in prairie gardens is that they don't take as long to grow to mature bulbs—and given that our growing season is disconcertingly short, they serve as a leg-up toward a harvest of decent-sized onions. You can direct sow them as soon as the ground has thawed—you don't need to start them indoors. Plus, they're gargantuan in size when compared with onion seeds, which makes them a breeze to sow.

When selecting onion sets, bear in mind that you may not be able to figure out the exact varieties you are getting. There are exceptions, but generally, "yellow" onions or "red" onions could be any number of varieties, all thrown together in one mesh bag. For some gardeners, this won't matter too much; for others there is a desire to know the exact varieties. Some gardeners want to grow onions of a particular flavour profile or that store better than others. If those qualities are important to you, then seed is definitely the way to go. You will always know the variety you are planting (unless your seeds are accidentally mixed together), you will have an incredible amount of different onions to choose from, and—in many cases—you will know the source of the seeds. The other thing to think about: Because bags of sets may be composed of more than one variety of onion, they may not all grow at uniform rates.

There is a fantastic trick to buying onion sets: Unlike the large, plump bulbs you're seeking out when you buy daffodils or tulips, small onion sets are best. The ones you really want will be about 1 inch (2.5 centimetres) in diameter, but most often you're not going to find such small ones for sale. In that case, it's best to simply judge the contents of the bags and buy the ones that are the smallest when compared to the others. The sets should be unblemished and properly filled out—not shrunken or shrivelled or dried husks. The smaller sets are better at successfully producing large healthy mature bulbs at summer's end.

Onion seeds, on the other hand, take aeons to grow. (Well, not quite, but they do take a very long time.) Most varieties take at least three weeks simply to germinate. On the prairies, it is definitely recommended to sow onion seed indoors. Depending on your location, early March is usually the time to seriously start thinking about setting them up. Occasionally, germination can be spotty with onion seeds, so sow a few more than you think you'll need—even if they all come up, you'll be happy for the extras at harvest time.

If you don't want to grow your own onions from seeds and you're not keen on sets, you can occasionally find onion transplants available in garden centres in the spring. These can be sown as soon as the ground can be worked and the danger of frost has passed. As with seeds, there are a lot of varieties of onion transplants.

If you're not looking to harvest mature bulbs, you can grow any onion sets or seed just for the greens.

One final tip: If you purchase onion sets and can't get them into the ground right away, store them in a cool, dry spot. High heat and humidity will promote mould.—SN

Choose small, unblemished onion sets for planting.

The seed catalogue lists long-day, day-neutral, and short-day onions—what types are best for prairie gardeners to grow?

For many plants, the number of daylight hours and hours of darkness per day influences their development, as well as spurs the production of flowers and fruit. This response of plants to changes in day length is called photoperiodism. If you've ever grown a poinsettia and tried to get it to rebloom, you'll know something about how this works. To put it concisely, short-day plants need at least twelve hours of darkness per day to promote blooming and/or fruiting. Long-day plants require less than twelve hours of darkness each day. Day-neutral plants will bloom or produce fruit with little regard for the day length, although longer daylight hours may result in more prolific blooms or increase yields.

For prairie gardeners, we're usually looking to grow either day-neutral or long-day onions. In the summer, when our daylight lasts considerably more than twelve hours, onions steadily form up plump bulbs. (Gardeners in the southern United States, on the other hand, cannot grow long-day onions—they simply do not have enough daylight hours for bulbs to form.)

While we can certainly grow short-day onions on the prairies, the bulbs often form too quickly and may not reach the size we would like to see.[2] —SN

Is it worth it to grow leeks on the prairies? How can I grow some that are larger than the size of my index finger?

Part of the difficulty with growing leeks is that they require a long growing season, which we really don't have on the prairies. For that reason, it is not recommended to direct sow leeks into the garden: Start them indoors in February or March (depending on where you live). When considering the timeline, don't forget to factor in that leek seed takes two to three weeks to germinate, and you'll want to add in a short hardening-off period before transplanting them. If you have a choice, select cultivars with the shortest days to maturity time, so that you have a better chance at getting a decent harvest before the snow flies.

Before you get your leek transplants in the garden, make sure your soil is amended with aged compost. You don't want a massive nitrogen dump, as that will only promote leafy growth, but the soil should be in good shape nutritionally. Be prepared to offer leeks regular, consistent moisture — they will be underwhelming performers

The key to a good leek harvest is time, and plenty of it! Start plants indoors for transplanting as soon as the soil warms.

if you skimp on the water, and they may be prone to mould and other issues if you overindulge them.

Probably the most notable characteristic of leeks is the way they're grown, with the blanched stems and the upright, slightly leathery green leaves above the soil line. Although you can eat all parts of the plant, the white stems are the most desirable for cooking. To keep the appealing white stems, they must be deprived of sunlight. This is usually accomplished through hilling the plants. As the stems grow, gently mound soil around them. Be careful not to pile soil into the base of the leaves—sloppy hilling will only lead to gritty leeks, and no one wants that! Keep hilling throughout the summer as the stems get taller.

If you don't want to hill your leek plants, there is an alternative. Save toilet paper or paper towel rolls and place them right over top of the seedlings once they've been transplanted in-ground. Sink the rolls so that the tops of the rolls are no higher than the base of the leaves. The leek stems will keep growing inside the rolls and no sunlight will reach them as long as you periodically adjust the heights of the rolls to compensate for the new growth. (You may find it necessary to tape two toilet paper rolls together lengthwise before putting them into place.) The rolls can be composted at the end of the season.—SN

The lowdown on soil

Most vegetables have similar needs when it comes to the type of soil they grow best in. Check off the requirements on this list for top results:

* ✳ Moisture retentive but well-draining
* ✳ No weeds
* ✳ Bacterial-dominated, not fungal-dominated. This means that the majority of the soil's biomass—a source of energy derived from organic materials—is taken up with bacteria, not fungi. Bacterial-dominated soils are good for growing food crops, whereas fungal-dominated soils are often found in forested areas.[3] To boost the bacterial dominance in your soil, amendments containing nitrogen are favoured. (Compost, compost, and more compost!)[4]

When is it time to harvest garlic, onions, and shallots?

For all three of these delicious alliums, harvest time occurs in late summer or early autumn, when the tops begin to turn yellow and dry out. Some of the tops may begin to fall over. Let this happen naturally—don't bend the tops over.

Do not cut the tops off when you harvest the plants—dig them up with the leaves intact. For long-term storage, garlic, onions, and shallots must be cured.[5]

If you're keen on harvesting garlic before it matures and produces bulbs, you can do so. If sown outdoors the previous autumn, green garlic—which resembles scallions

This beauty is waiting to be served up in a tasty meal.

(green onions)—can be pulled for eating in late spring. (Alternatively, you can sow garlic bulbs as soon as the soil warms in the spring for an early summer harvest.) Some gardeners like to grow green garlic in containers indoors, for use year-round. It may be continuously sown from cloves or bulbils (seeds). Use it up right away in your favourite recipes, as it doesn't store long.

As an interesting aside, we've occasionally been asked how to grow and harvest black garlic. Black garlic is not grown; it is created. A long period of low temperatures and humidity causes the enzymes in regular garlic to undergo a chemical process, which breaks them down and creates a new, unique flavour that is highly prized in cooking.[6]—SN

Brassicas

4

Why did my broccoli or cauliflower plants fail to produce heads?

Growing broccoli and cauliflower can be tricky!

Like many vegetables in the Brassicaceae family, both broccoli and cauliflower are cool-season crops. Seedlings should be transplanted early, as soon as your soil has warmed up, between 39 and 45°F (4 to 7°C).[1] Do make sure to properly harden off seedlings purchased from a greenhouse, as they will surely need to toughen up before being exposed to our weather. Seedlings should be covered with floating row covers or cloches to protect them while they settle in or if another late shot of colder temperatures occurs. The seedlings will love the cooler soil and temperatures and take off.

It is the extremes of heat and cold, along with dry soil, that will stress broccoli and cauliflower plants early in their development and impact their ability to form heads, all unfortunately common occurrences during prairie springs. In particular, lack of consistent moisture in the soil, lack of abundant nutrients, and soil pH levels being on the alkaline side will tie up nutrients so that they are not available to be taken up by the plants, which will result in lack of head formation.

Beyond the unpredictable weather in early spring, there are other potential causes for failure to produce heads at all. *Brassica* plants generally have weak root systems, and both broccoli and cauliflower are subject to root damage from being root-bound in small seedling trays, where roots dry out from being in too little soil or simply from being in a small space for too long. Additionally, it is easy to damage the roots of seedlings when transplanting them. Both crops need to be well spaced to avoid overcrowding, with the resulting stress caused by undue competition for water, nutrients, light, air circulation, and room for good root growth.

Sometimes both broccoli and cauliflower will form heads, but they will "button," a term that means that the heads failed to grow and will remain tight and small throughout the season. Buttoning can occur if the developing plants experience unseasonably cold temperatures once head formation begins. It is wise to always pay heed to incoming cold fronts and have floating row covers handy to cover the plants, as needed. If your broccoli and cauliflower plants have buttoned, you can remove the tiny growths and eat them. The plants might eventually produce some small heads as side shoots, so you may be able to salvage something out of them in time.

Do consider growing these crops, along with cabbage, kale, collards and kohlrabi, in polytunnels throughout the growing season to help provide a consistent and as stress-free a growing environment as possible. Mulching once seedlings are well established will also serve to keep roots cooler and maintain valuable soil moisture.[2]—JM AND SN

This broccoli plant is producing plenty of side shoots.

What causes cabbage heads to split?
What about kohlrabi?

Properly timed watering practices are the key to lovely kohlrabi and cabbage.

It's all about the H_2O!

As cabbage heads form up, they become dense and solid. At this point, if they are given a lot of water, either from supplemental irrigation or from heavy rainfall, they may crack open. It's pretty much impossible to control the weather, but you can definitely watch your watering to prevent this from occurring. An oft-used method to prevent cabbages from splitting—cutting or breaking the roots—will sometimes work, but it damages the plant and necessitates an early harvest.[3]

With kohlrabi, drought and heat stress are partly to blame when the round, enlarged stems split. Maintain even, consistent moisture for the best-tasting kohlrabi. If possible, shade the plants during long periods of high heat. A simple protective structure may be made from wooden stakes and polyethylene shade cloth (available in some garden centres and wherever greenhouse supplies are sold).

Finally, ensure your soil is not compacted and heavy. Kohlrabi will be less likely to split if the roots are free to take up water and nutrients from the soil. Plus, the stems will taste better, too! Amending the soil with compost over several seasons is the best treatment for compacted soils.[4]—SN

How do I keep my radishes from getting woody and tasteless?

Subpar radishes are a result of several factors, most of them controllable on the gardener's end. Be sure to harvest radishes when they are young and tender—don't wait too long or the roots will suffer in taste and texture. Woody radishes also occur when the soil is too dry or if supplemental irrigation has not been consistent. Stick to a regular watering schedule and mulch the bases of the plants with clean straw for best results. The one difficult thing to control is the temperature: Radishes will underperform during periods of prolonged heat. Plant them early in the spring, as soon as the ground is warm enough to work, or late in the summer for a fall crop. —SN

Don't allow radishes to linger in the ground. Pull them and enjoy them as soon as they are ready.

What is the key to successfully growing decent-sized Brussels sprouts? Mine are way too small.

These Brussels sprouts are just the right size for harvesting.

The Brussels sprouts you typically purchase in the grocery store are usually slightly larger than two inches (five centimetres) in diameter, but most home gardeners usually pick them a bit before they reach that size. If the plants are producing only tiny, pea-sized sprouts, however, there are a few things you can do to help them enlarge.

It is not recommended to direct sow Brussels sprouts in our prairie gardens—you simply don't have time to grow most cultivars to a harvestable size before winter arrives. You need to be able to pick them in September in our climate (sometimes you'll be fortunate and be able to harvest them well into October). Start the plants indoors in early to mid-April for early cultivars (90–110 days) and in late February or early March for cultivars that require more time. Remember to factor in a hardening-off period before transplanting outdoors in May! Offering Brussels sprouts seedlings a head start encourages sprout production far earlier than if you direct sow, which may lead to larger sprouts.[5]

Don't skimp on the water, and don't offer it in irregular intervals. Brussels sprouts need consistent moisture for plump, tender, sweet sprouts. Flavour, texture, and size are compromised if you fail to maintain a regular watering schedule.

A traditional practice that some gardeners—and even some (usually small-scale) commercial growers—occasionally use is to top the plants. In order to force the plants into focusing on enlarging the sprouts, a maximum of two inches (five centimetres) of growth is cut off at the very top of the stalks. Timing is everything with topping. If you choose to go this route, it is generally advised to top the plants approximately one month before the date of harvest. (Of course, factors such as weather, diseases, or pests may contribute to altering the timeline, but you can predict the harvest date by examining your seed package.) The sprouts form on the stalks from the bottom upwards, so if the timing seems correct and the bottom sprouts have reached a minimum size of 1 inch (2.5 centimetres) in diameter, you can try topping the plants. Topping them too early may actually reduce yields. Instead of focusing on the sprouts, the plants may start to branch out of the cut area.[6] It may require a bit of experimentation over several years and crops to determine if topping is the right strategy for you; there may be no need to do it at all, especially when growing early cultivars. Plus, if you don't top the plants, you can eat the upper leaves as you would a cabbage!—SN

Sunlight and siting

All plants have preferences when it comes to the amount of sunlight they need to thrive, and to set flowers and fruit. Here is a key to deciphering the differences between those little sunlight symbols on your plant labels:

* ✳ FULL SUN: Direct sunlight for six or more hours
* ✳ PART SHADE: Two to four hours of direct sunlight
* ✳ FILTERED (DAPPLED) SHADE: Sunlight is indirect, filtered through the canopies of nearby deciduous trees
* ✳ FULL SHADE: Less than two hours of direct sunlight (the rest of the time, sunlight is filtered; this does not mean the site is in complete darkness—plants won't grow in such a location)

Carrots, Celery,
Beets, and Lettuce

5

What causes "sunburning" in carrots? How can I prevent this?

Keeping carrots covered in soil may prevent sunburning.

Sometimes during the course of the growing season, carrot roots (and those of beets, turnips, radishes, and other root vegetables) will lift themselves out of the ground so that the tops of the roots are exposed. When the sunlight hits these bare spots, chlorophyll is produced and the crowns of the roots turn green. It's perfectly safe to eat the carrot parts that exhibit this green sunburn, but the flavour isn't fantastic — it tends to be a bit on the bitter side. You can just cut these parts off before eating.

If you want to prevent sunburning from occurring, just pile a bit of soil onto the tops of the carrot roots when you notice them poking up. — SN

I'm having really spotty carrot germination. What can I do to prevent this next year?

Carrot seed is super tiny, and if planted too deeply, it may not germinate. Try to sow seed only about 1/4 inch (6 millimetres) deep and give them just the barest of soil cover. The use of seed tape may make for easier sowing, as the seeds are held in place by the tape, which is biodegradable. Another bonus: The seeds in seed tape are precisely spaced so they make for less thinning later on. Pelleted seed is another option: The seeds are coated in a type of clay to make them easier to sow evenly. (The clay does not contain any chemicals or other treatments.)

As with any other plant seed that is getting ready to germinate, consistent, even moisture is essential. Don't let them dry out too much between waterings. Likewise, never offer too much water, which can encourage issues such as mould. A traditional method of inspiring seeds to get going involves laying a wooden board (or tacking a piece of burlap) over the top of the newly planted seed. This helps to hold the moisture in the soil. Frequently check beneath the board or cloth, and once the seed has sprouted, you can remove it.

Heavy clay soils can make germination tricky for seeds such as carrots. Your soil should be friable (also known as "delightfully crumbly," but not dry and powdery). Regular amendments with compost will help soil texture, not to mention fertility.

Finally, carrots can take up to three weeks to germinate, so don't worry too much if they don't poke out before then. They're more than worth the wait.—SN

*These carrots are perfectly edible,
but the soil may not have been
properly prepared before planting.*

My carrots are puny or — even worse — forked or crooked! What can I do to prevent this?

Fortunately, these are usually easy problems to correct. Not preparing the soil properly before planting carrots (or parsnips, for that matter) can cause misshapen roots. Heavy compaction or clay in the soil can be an issue. Amend with compost to improve soil, but don't rely on a single application to do the job. This is a task that will have to be undertaken over several growing seasons.

If your soil contains rocks, and the placement of them is just so, your carrots will end up working around them, resulting in forked roots. Be sure to remove any rocks found in your soil.

Planting seeds too closely or sowing too thickly will guarantee twisted, tiny carrots. We recommend thinning the seedlings when they are about two inches (five centimetres) tall and sporting one or two sets of true leaves.

Insufficient or inconsistent watering will also affect carrot growth. Keep up with the supplemental irrigation, if conditions are dry, but be careful not to overwater.

Ensuring your bed is weed-free is important as well — carrots do not appreciate any sort of competition for space, water, or nutrients.

Very occasionally, carrots will fork due to the feeding of northern root-knot nematodes (*Meloidogyne hapla*), a type of roundworm. We usually think of nematodes as beneficial to the garden, but there are a few species that can damage plants. The eggs of these tiny roundworms can overwinter in the soil in our cold climate and hatch when the soil warms in the spring. The juvenile and adult forms actively feed on the roots of some plant species, including carrots. Galls may form on the roots, affecting the uptake of nutrients and water to the plant. For the most part, however, we would look for other causes for "ugly" carrots, as they are more likely.[1] — SN

Is there anything I can do so that my celery plants produce larger bunches?

We'll say it up front: Celery is not the easiest vegetable to grow. It requires significant and consistent inputs of water and nutrients for success. Seed takes up to three weeks to germinate and then can take upwards of three months to grow plants with sizable bunches of stalks (which, botanically, are actually elongated petioles—the plant parts that attach the leaves to a stem). On top of all that, celery doesn't really like hot weather, so getting it through summer can sometimes be a challenge. Too much heat can affect the flavour of the stalks, rendering them bitter. To make things even more interesting, if you transplant celery too early in the season, when the soil and ambient temperatures are still cool, the plants may quickly flower and go to seed in response to the stress.

Can you win? Yes, you can! To increase your chances of harvesting big delicious bunches of celery, try growing them from transplants instead of seeds. You'll have a bit of a leg up by shortening the time to maturity. Because celery takes so long to germinate, you'll want to start seeds no later than mid- to late February indoors (to transplant at the end of May). It is extremely important that the seedlings have a strong root system before planting outside—weak plants are not likely to offer much come harvest time.

Ensure your planting beds are amended with aged compost before sowing or transplanting celery.

Unlike many plants that crave space, celery likes to be squished, just a little—it encourages the stalks to grow tall. Plants should be spaced about twelve inches (thirty centimetres) apart.

Watering is perhaps the most important thing you can do for your celery plants. Water them a lot, and water them often. That's not to say you should drown them—you absolutely should not—but consistent, even moisture is the difference between stringy celery and the good stuff. Taste is altered by inconsistent moisture as well— and not for the better. Some gardeners use drip irrigation in their celery beds, which we definitely recommend to help keep up with these

Growing celery from transplants instead of direct sowing can be helpful!

thirsty plants. Mulching the bases of the plants with straw is also helpful, as it will help maintain soil moisture.

As a side note: Did you know that you don't have to harvest the whole bunch of celery at once? This practice is not exactly conducive to obtaining large bunches, but celery may be treated as a cut-and-come-again crop. Outer stalks may be harvested, a few at a time, when needed. Just break them off at the base, being careful not to crack the entire plant from the roots. Allow the plant to keep growing. You can keep taking individual stalks from the outside edges, whenever they are ready, or stop and wait until the bunch is large enough to harvest all at once.

When it comes time to harvest your celery, avoid picking on hot, dry days, as wilting isn't appealing (for neither you nor the celery!).[2]—SN

My beets are tiny and I've been growing them all season. How can I fix this issue for next year?

For gorgeous beets like these, thin your plants early in the season.

Beet seed is pretty cool: Most cultivars are a multigerm type, which means that each little lump you hold in your hand is actually a fruit containing multiple small seeds (usually between two and five). You can't separate them before planting, so you throw the whole thing in the ground as one "seed." (Another common veggie that has multigerm seed is Swiss chard.) Of course, this means that when the seed germinates, the seedlings are all way too close to one another. Thinning the plants when they have gained two sets of true leaves or are about 3 inches (7.5 centimetres) tall will give each plant the space it needs. Pulling the thinnings up will only dislodge the roots of the keepers, so use a pair of long-bladed scissors to cut each unwanted plant at its base. (Don't forget to save the ones you clip and throw them in a salad!) Leave at least 3 inches (7.5 centimetres) of space between plants. This will help the roots plump up nicely for a later harvest.

Another thing to watch for is a high nitrogen content in your soil. This will cause beets to grow beautiful leafy tops, but will fail to produce much underground. If you use compost in your beet bed, make sure it is well aged.

Maintain a regular watering schedule when growing beets, as this will also help root development. Water consistently, and do not allow the plants to become too dry between waterings.[3]

Finally, the cultivars you choose to plant can make a difference! There are beets grown specifically for their tops, not the roots. These include 'Merlin', 'Fresh Start', and 'Fresh Pak'. If you're looking to make borscht, don't select those. Other beets may have slender cylindrical roots instead of large globular ones. —SN

Which vegetables are better to directly sow into the garden (not start as transplants)?

Despite our short growing season on the prairies, some crops don't need to be started indoors, as they have plenty of time to produce a good harvest if directly sown into the ground once the soil and ambient temperatures are warm enough.

As a general rule, all root crops should be directly sown. For instance, I have never managed to transplant a carrot seedling!

A secondary rule is that any crop that is ready to harvest within two months should be directly sown, as it makes little sense to devote the energy, time, and resources to sow them indoors, except if you are looking for a quick jump on the season or are practising intensive succession planting. Radishes, corn salad, and spinach all fall within this category.

Thirdly, some species have weak or easily disturbed root systems that do not take kindly to transplanting. Beans and peas really don't enjoy the process of transplanting, so you disturb them less if you plant them where they will grow. Even cucumbers and zucchini prefer to be directly sown.

All this being said, this list is merely a guideline, and if you really want to start these crops indoors or prefer to purchase seedlings, go for it!

* Arugula
* Beans
* Beets
* Carrots
* Corn
* Corn salad (mâche)
* Cucumbers
* Endive
* Garlic
* Kohlrabi
* Lettuce
* Mustard greens
* Onion sets
* Parsnips
* Peas
* Potatoes
* Radishes
* Rutabagas
* Spinach
* Turnips
* Winter squash, such as pumpkin and butternut
* Zucchini and other summer squash

NOTE: In very short-season gardens, sowing seeds indoors to transplant as seedlings for some of these crops makes sense, so that there is a chance that they will reach maturity before the nights become colder and longer and the season ends in an abrupt and unwelcome way.

Parsnips do not transplant well and should be directly sown.

What causes heading lettuce to fail to produce heads?

The attraction of head lettuce is its packed, ball-shaped cluster of leaves that you harvest in one go. Because you have to wait for it to form heads, head lettuce can take a bit longer than leaf lettuce to reach a harvestable stage, and, along the way, a few factors may influence whether or not it actually produces a head.

Temperature can be an issue. Anything consistently warmer than 64°F (18°C), especially if the nighttime temperatures do not drop below that, may cause it to bolt. Drought

Don't crowd head lettuce in the garden—it needs room to form beautiful heads.

is another problem. Head lettuce—actually, lettuce in general—requires consistent, even moisture. Do not overwater at any time, as that can promote disease and reduce yield.

Make sure you're planting lettuce in well-drained soil. Soil with a high clay content is not recommended. Don't forget to amend the soil with compost before planting. Offering optimum conditions will encourage heading.

Spacing is critical as well. Head lettuce needs a little extra room: ten to fourteen inches (twenty-five to thirty-six centimetres) apart is a good idea. (You can squish leaf lettuce in a little tighter than that.)[4] —SN

My lettuce is brown at the edges of the leaves—why?

This condition is called tipburn. It can happen with both head and leaf lettuces and results in blemished produce and a reduced shelf life. Certain types of tipburn—particularly those found in the lettuce heart or inner leaves—may be caused by a calcium deficiency, but don't go running out to the garden to add calcium to your soil: Chances are your soil is just fine. Lettuce roots take up calcium from the soil along with water. One of the functions of calcium in plants is to nourish cell walls, which it cannot do if it is not being transported through the plant. When calcium is not available, the cell walls weaken and discolour. You can resolve this problem by supplying consistent, even applications of water throughout the entire life of the plant.

Tipburn on the outer leaves can also be caused by drying, strong winds. If this is an issue, plant lettuce in a less exposed area or protect plants with row covers.

Fortunately, if your lettuce suffers a small amount of tipburn, you can just tear the brown edges off and eat the rest of the leaf.[5]—SN

Peas, Beans, and Corn

6

Pea pod problems: They're empty, dry, or completely absent. Why is this happening?

First, let's talk pea types, as knowing the differences will help answer these questions. The pods of snow and snap peas are harvested and eaten whole—you don't shell them. Snap pea pods will typically have tiny peas inside, but snow peas are harvested before peas develop. If you are growing garden (or shelling) peas, however, you should expect peas inside them, as that's the part you want to eat.

If the peas inside the pods of your garden peas are non-existent or too small, it is usually due to the pods being picked too early. You'll know when garden peas are ready to harvest when the pods are cylindrical in shape (not flat). Extreme moisture levels can play a role in pod development as well: Too much or too little water can be detrimental.

One reason why pea pods (and the peas inside) might dry out is a lack of water while the plants are producing fruit. Ensure you maintain a regular watering schedule to prevent this from occurring.

The existence of dry pea pods can also be related to either the gardener's vacation time or an overwhelmingly busy schedule. Garden peas need to be harvested on time, if you want to enjoy the finest sweet flavour of green peas. If you wait too long, the sugars in the peas quickly turn into tasteless pulpy starches.

If you do happen to leave your peas on the vines for too long, it isn't a complete waste. Those dry peas inside the pods? They are pea soup waiting to happen. They are also seeds to save for planting next year.

If pods do not appear on your pea plants at all, check your soil nutrients. If you are offering them too much nitrogen, you could be boosting leafy growth and little else. Another reason for a lack of pods may be due to poor fertilization. Peas are self-pollinating, but every so often, when temperatures fluctuate dramatically, fertilization doesn't occur. You can help the transfer of pollen along by gently shaking the plants when the flowers are in bloom. As well, during periods of high heat, we recommend shading plants to try to regulate temperatures.

These peas were left unpicked and are no longer good for fresh eating.

Plants may fail to produce pods during prolonged periods of drought. Offer consistent supplemental irrigation when required.[1] —SN

My bean plants didn't produce well this year. What can I do to get more beans?

There are several reasons why beans may not produce a lot of pods (or any at all). Beans are self-pollinating , but the trouble may lie in pollen transfer. Help out by gently shaking the plants to distribute the pollen from the anther to the stigma.

Sometimes the blossoms may drop before fruit is produced. Temperature extremes (consistently hot or cold over many days) and fluctuations can cause this to happen. If you have a greenhouse — or the budget to build one — the indoor growing conditions may offer more stable temperatures than the great (too cold or too hot) outdoors. You can also try shading plants from excessive heat by building a tent structure using stakes and shade cloth. Beans grown in containers may be moved into a more sheltered location during periods of high heat.

Healthy beans like this can be achieved by paying attention to soil and light conditions.

Site beans in a spot in your garden that receives full sun; too much shade may cause the flowers to fall off.

If your beans are producing flowers but very little fruit, it may be related to soil conditions. Although beans do require fertile soil, too much nitrogen tends to favour leafy growth over fruit production, so dial back the high-nitrogen fertilizer.

Finally, if you're not picking bean pods when they're ready to harvest, choosing to leave them on the plants may prevent new ones from forming.[2] —SN

Which veggies can grow in part shade or filtered (dappled) shade?

Radicchio can tolerate partial shade.

Dappled shade is defined as two to four hours per day of direct sun (with the rest of the time out of direct sunlight). Most veggie plants prefer six or more hours of direct sunlight to achieve mature size and productivity. Those vegetables grown in partial shade are usually smaller, and may be less productive in terms of leaves, flowers, and fruit produced.

Some vegetable plants actually prefer partial shade, where the sunlight is less intense, produce tasty produce grown in less stressful conditions, and will not bolt as quickly as they may do in hotter conditions. You will know if your vegetable plants are not getting enough sunlight to thrive as they will appear to be struggling, may be leaning toward the sunlight, and will be subject to more pests.

As a rule, leafy vegetables perform best in partial to dappled shade, veggies with roots may tolerate some shade, and fruits do not like shade at all.

These vegetables, which prefer morning light or partial shade, are harvested before reaching mature size and are milder and more succulent.

* Amaranth
* Arugula
* Bok choi
* Corn salad (mâche)
* Endive and escarole
* Lettuce
* Mustard greens, including mizuna, komatsuna, and tatsoi
* New Zealand spinach
* Radicchio
* Spinach
* Watercress

These vegetables will tolerate morning light or partial shade. Though they will grow slower if they are not in direct sun, they will often be milder in taste and less likely to bolt. However, in short-season growing zones, growing in the shade may delay maturity to the extent that frost may come before the crop is mature.

* Beets
* Broccoli
* Cabbage
* Cauliflower
* Kale
* Kohlrabi
* Leeks
* Radishes
* Swiss chard[3]

Factors such as drought can affect the yield of corn plants.

What causes sweet corn to produce just a few ears? I was hoping for a better harvest.

There are several factors that can reduce yields for corn. Soil moisture levels on either extreme—excessively wet or too dry—can be a huge issue. Drought can result in uneven germination or can cause emerging plants to become stunted, or worse, to stop growing altogether. Too much moisture can actually reduce the ability of corn plants to take on the macronutrients they need to produce large plump ears. Cool temperatures over a period of several days or huge temperature swings from cold to hot can also reduce yields. Corn is a heat-lover (like many gardeners we know!).

Herbicide damage from overspraying can harm plants and affect production. It is recommended to manually control weeds by hand-picking them.

A lack of pollination is a possibility as well. Corn is a monoecious plant. This means that each plant possesses both female and male reproductive organs. Male and female flowers must bloom at almost the same time, so that pollination—and, hopefully, fertilization!—will successfully occur. Corn is wind-pollinated, so plants need to be planted in close proximity to each other to facilitate the transfer of pollen. Sowing in a grid pattern instead of a single long row is the preferred method.

Finally, some corn cultivars produce higher yields than others. In trials done by the University of Saskatchewan in 2011, the cultivars 'Luscious', 'Polka', 'Pow-wow', and 'Big Jim' were found to have excellent yields. Of course, these rates take into account specific weather conditions, soil types, and other influencing factors. More corn cultivars are being developed all the time, so have fun experimenting with them and find your favourites![4]—SN

I am looking at the seed catalogue and there are so many categories of sweet corn. What are the differences between them?

In a nutshell, the selective breeding of sweet corn over centuries has brought us to the present-day hybrids, which have been specifically chosen for their flavour, texture, and storage capabilities. This gives us a number of categories of sweet corn to grow, which may lead to confusion and hamper decision-making when it comes time to order seeds. (Plus, the categories are usually referenced as initials, which can be really weird if you don't know what on earth the initials stand for.)

* **su (Standard or Sugary):** This type of sweet corn is likely the closest to what was grown several decades ago. It is not as sweet as other types (it tastes like "corn," if that makes sense — and that's not a bad thing!). Its sugar content falls somewhere between 8 and 18 percent. The texture of su corn is a bit chewier than other types. Unfortunately, su corn doesn't store very well; you almost have to use it on the same day it is picked, as the sugars in the kernels quickly convert to starches. A drawback of this is that when it's time to harvest, you have to move! Su corn should be picked all at once. (Fortunately, it stands up very well to freezing and canning.) The really great thing about su corn, however, is that you can sow it in cooler soils than other types of corn — it doesn't mind as much.

* **se (Sugar Enhanced):** This type of corn is made up of 30 to 35 percent sugars. It may be stored for longer periods of time than su corn. Just to make things interesting, there is also a Fully Sugary Enhanced hybrid, which contains a bit more sugar, but not quite as much as the sh2 hybrid.

* **sh2 (Supersweet or Shrunken-2):** First of all, because we're certain inquiring minds want to know, the Shrunken-2 moniker refers to the fact that this type of corn has dry kernels that are small and wrinkled. The kernels are much sweeter than su corn (40 to 50 percent sugars), and sh2 corn stores for longer periods of time. The cost of this comes in yield — sh2 corn usually doesn't produce as much as su corn.

* **sy (Synergistic):** Finally, this sweet corn is a combination of se + sh2, se + su, or se + su + sh2. (Ah, genetics!) There is plenty of sugar to be had here, and the kernels are juicy. For success, sow sy corn in warm soil.

Choose the type of sweet corn you want to grow based on the qualities that you are most interested in. The most important thing to look for in the seed catalogue is the days-to-harvest number: You must have enough time during our short growing season to bring this crop from seed to table.[5] —SN

Try growing different types of corn until you find your favourites.

Tomatoes and Peppers

7

A lack of pollination can affect tomato flowers.

What causes tomato flowers to prematurely drop off?

Blossom drop is a fairly common occurrence in tomatoes, and you may see it sometimes in beans and some other vegetables as well.

The biggest culprit is a lack of pollination. One simple way to help plants along is to very gently shake the stems to help transfer the pollen. Do not shake too hard or you'll knock the flowers off, due to sheer force. Some gardeners will actually just gently blow on the flowers instead—it's a bit more peaceful. These methods sound strange, but they are useful because tomatoes are self-fertile and have both male and female parts on each flower. If you aren't keen on the extra work and prefer pollinator insects to help your tomato plants along, welcome them into your garden by not using pesticides, and situate tomato plants near attractive, high-pollen, and high-nectar plants such as borage, calendula, bee balm (*Monarda*), and anise hyssop.

Other factors are environmental. Temperature fluctuations, from high heat to extreme cold, can be a big problem. Depending on where you live on the prairies, the swing in temperatures from hot days to downright chilly nights may contribute to a good night's sleep for you, but tomato flowers aren't too keen about it.

Extremely low or high humidity may also be an issue. It turns out pollen doesn't like to stick if the humidity isn't just right.

Finally, too much nitrogen-based fertilizer can also shorten the length of time tomatoes retain their blooms. Don't completely forgo the nitrogen, because tomatoes need some, but don't focus on it when you fertilize tomatoes.[1]—SN

*Knowing which type of
tomato plants you are growing
determines pruning practices.*

What is the difference between indeterminate and determinate tomatoes?

In theory, indeterminate tomatoes are supposed to keep growing indefinitely, but, of course, cultural and environmental factors play into this. Indeterminate tomatoes will grow tall, and they will sprawl if you fail to trellis or stake them with a substantial support system. Indeterminate tomatoes flower on side shoots that grow up the entire length of the plants' stems. They usually (but not always) have better yields than determinate tomatoes, as they produce fruit over a longer period of time.

Determinate tomatoes are "bushier" when compared to indeterminate tomatoes. They grow wide instead of tall. Gardeners will often support determinate tomatoes with the thin wire cages found at garden centres, and, most of the time, that's sufficient. Determinate tomato plants grow to a certain height and then stop once their terminal (flowering) buds have developed. These plants produce one big crop all season—usually earlier than indeterminate varieties—and all the tomatoes ripen around the same time. Sometimes the plants will continue to produce a bit more fruit until the season is finished, but the yield is far less than the initial bounty.

You don't hear about them too often, but there are also semi-determinate tomatoes. These grow both tall and bushy, and they require support.

Dwarf tomatoes are yet another option, very popular with small-space gardeners. They seldom reach heights more than three feet (ninety centimetres).

Why should you know what type of tomato you're growing? Knowing the growth habits and size your plants will reach at maturity is useful if you have space restrictions. It also helps you decide what type of support to use for the plants. Most importantly, if you are considering pruning your tomatoes, you should pursue the task only if you know the way in which they are growing. Yield may be affected if you prune the wrong type.[2]—SN

Do you have to prune the side shoots from tomatoes? If so, when and how do you do it?

The general consensus is that pruning away the side shoots (or suckers) of tomato plants has immense benefits. It may not be quite that simple, however, especially for prairie gardeners.

First of all, only indeterminate tomato plants are candidates for pruning. Leave determinate, semi-determinate, and dwarf tomato plants alone, as pruning these types may lead to decreased yields. If you are purchasing plants in a garden centre or grabbing a package of seeds, the labelling should tell you what type of tomato plant you will be growing.

It is commonly believed that pruning indeterminate tomato plants will increase their yield, supposedly because all of that activity of producing more shoots and branches and flowers is exhausting for the plant. Tomato plants sucker naturally, however. They want to ensure that they make as much fruit as possible because each one contains numerous seeds, which might just be used to grow more tomatoes. Like all living species, they're all about reproduction. If you leave the side shoots on, the plants will simply keep working to produce more fruit, not less. The one thing that might happen if you don't prune your tomatoes is that the fruit may be smaller than that found on pruned plants.

If you wish to obtain the maximum size of fruit as determined by the variety you've planted, pruning may help. Leaving the suckers on will generate more branching and leafing, so pruning is also a good idea if the foliage of your plants is very dense, sprawling, or top-heavy. Pruning will help you control the growth or open up the crown so that more air can penetrate. (Good air circulation can help prevent or minimize the effects of certain diseases.) For many prairie gardeners, however, the growing season is so short that their tomato plants will never reach such lofty dimensions.

If you choose to prune, use a pair of small scissors (or your index finger and thumb) to carefully snip the side shoots that are emerging from the little crook just above the leaf branches. We recommend leaving a few shoots in place so that they can grow and flower (and hopefully set fruit), but it's up to you to decide how many shoots to get rid of. Remember that removing tomato suckers is an ongoing process throughout the growing season—they pop up very quickly on a healthy plant![3]

However, choosing not to prune can also be a huge benefit. Keeping more of the plant's leaves intact can help out on those super hot summer days when sunscald is a potential issue for your plants.—SN

Should I top my tomato plants to get better yields?

Most gardeners judiciously prune tomato plants instead of topping them, and honestly I'm not sure prairie tomato growers really need to top their plants, unless the vines are growing so absurdly out of control that there is no other option. An example of this would be if the plants are insanely top-heavy and the stems are breaking, or you cannot keep them off the ground.

If you are considering topping your tomato plants, remember that you can do so only on indeterminate types. Other types of tomato plants will not respond well to this sort of treatment and will negatively repay you with reduced yields.

Don't top mid-season, if possible—wait as long as you safely can. Topping will remove flowers and potential fruit from your plants, so doing it late in the season means that you (and your tomato plants) aren't wasting time on fruit that doesn't have enough time to develop and ripen.

To do the job: Choose the uppermost flowers and/or developing fruit that you are going to keep—these are going to be your "end points." Make your cuts above each of these points, removing the stem just above the leaf that sits closest to the flower/fruit that you've selected. Your tomato plants will keep growing after you've made these cuts, but they probably will not have time to produce flowers and fruit. In the meantime, you don't have to worry about your plants collapsing under their own weight, and you can get ready to harvest the end-of-the-season fruit![4]—SN

My tomatoes are mushy and rotting at the blossom end. What causes this?

Blossom-end rot (BER) is common in fruit-bearing edibles, such as tomatoes, cucumbers, zucchini and other summer squash, and peppers. It isn't caused by a pathogen or insect, but rather is influenced by a set of environmental conditions in our gardens during any particular year.

The symptoms of blossom-end rot show early as a light brown or tan area of discolouration at the blossom end of the fruit. Over the season, the patch will expand, darken, and become almost leathery. Inside, the flesh will become almost black. It is a shame to see. Although the portion not affected is perfectly edible, the taste may be less than stellar. I use any tomatoes so affected in soups and stews, after cutting away the damaged portions.

One of the primary causes of blossom-end rot is uneven watering, where the soil almost dries out, then is flooded with water. When the soil is dry, the plant cannot take up calcium, which is important for good fruit set. Uptake of calcium can also be inhibited if there is damage to roots through cultivation, or if the nitrogen levels in the soil are too high. Even planting in soil that is too cold can be a factor, as can soils with a pH factor too acidic or alkaline for some plants' liking. Low humidity is also a factor, as is too much sunlight and heat on the fruit. Occasionally the primary cause may be too little calcium in the soil.

Prevention then becomes a matter of good cultivation practices.

Buffer garden soils with liberal applications of compost, so that the soil's pH factor is as close to neutral as possible. Ensure that the soil is fertile with applications of fertilizer throughout the growing period. We prefer organic fish fertilizer, but there are many fertilizers available. For fruit-bearing plants, use a fertilizer low in nitrogen and higher in phosphorus and potassium, but one that also contains many of the trace elements required for healthy plants.

The key is to ensure plants get the type of calcium they need from the soil when given the proper amount of water, so that they can properly absorb it. Generations of gardeners have used amendments such as pulverized Tums or eggshells, and we recently heard of a time-honoured tradition of placing a whole egg in the bottom of a planting hole. Most prairie soils will contain enough calcium to satisfy plant needs; however, it's just a matter of getting it to them.

Everyone is always in a hurry to get tomato plants in the garden and growing, but it is wise to wait until the soil warms up. Tomatoes come from Central America, and they don't appreciate our cold soils. We wait until well past the last frost date before finally putting out our tomatoes. Once they are established, we recommend mulching around the plants both to conserve moisture in the soil and to keep the roots cooler.

The goal for watering is to ensure even soil moisture at all times. Whether your plants are in containers or in the ground, the soil should be moist right through the soil profile. Using water spikes or ollas (unglazed clay pots) for in-soil water diffusion is an excellent method to both conserve water and ensure that it is where it should be — right next to the plants' roots.

Finally, if you find that blossom-end rot is a recurring problem, despite your best efforts, look for varieties that are less prone to BER, such as the heart-shaped 'Oxheart', and smaller ones, such as cherry or grape tomatoes. There are also cultivars that have been bred specifically to be less prone to blossom-end rot.[5] — JM

The key to prevention of blossom-end rot is careful watering practices.

Does changing the pH of my soil make my tomatoes taste sweeter?

Tomatoes do not like growing in extremely acidic soils, but in most places on the prairies, that is not an issue—if anything, our soils tend to be on the alkaline side. Unless a soil test indicates that your soil is in need of a correction, don't worry about it. And there is no need to add any other "magical" ingredients to the soil, such as Epsom salts, granulated sugar, or baking soda . . . the secret to sweet-tasting tomatoes lies in the plant's genetics. Look for and grow sweet-tasting cultivars—and have fun experimenting with new ones each year until you find your favourites.—SN

One of the best things about finding the sweetest selections of tomatoes is the taste test!

What causes bleached, dry areas on the developing fruit of peppers? What can I do to prevent this?

It's fairly common knowledge that pepper plants love the heat, but occasionally, enough is enough! When signs of sunscald appear on pepper fruit (or, for that matter, the foliage), it's time to take action. The scorch marks left by too much sunlight may make the skin of severely damaged fruit leathery, tough, and tasteless. The fruit may begin to crack open, and the fissures may allow bacteria and other potential problems to further exacerbate an already bad situation. (Pepper fruit that is not heavily affected by sunscald may be perfectly fine to eat—it will simply appear blemished. Don't throw it away unless it becomes mushy and gross!)

Use shade cloth and stakes to protect individual plants, or create a hoop tunnel covered in shade cloth for larger crops. Plants that have lost a portion of their crowns due to pests and diseases may be more prone to sunscald, as the fruit isn't shaded by the leaves. Provide optimal light, water, nutrients, appropriate soil conditions, and siting to minimize plant stress.[6]—SN

What does it mean when a chili pepper shows "corks"?

Corking in peppers is a term that refers to superficial cracking of the outer skin. The resulting thin white striations look like the wavy lines on a cork. Corking is the pepper equivalent of stretch marks in humans—indicators of a growth spurt brought on by a sudden increase in heat and water.

Corking may be prevented by maintaining a regular, consistent watering schedule. Pepper plants often perform well if grown in a greenhouse setting where temperatures are easier to control.

Corking does not diminish the flavour of the blemished peppers; in fact, some cooks claim it actually increases the amount of capsicum they contain, which makes them hotter. (So far, there aren't any scientific studies to back up that statement, so we will leave you to conduct your own taste tests.) Bell (sweet) peppers may also cork, but it happens more often with chilies.

Peppers that exhibit corking should be harvested within a few days. The skin may split if the peppers are left too long on the plants.

Splitting may also be caused if peppers undergo a period of drought, followed by significant rainfall, or a large amount of supplemental irrigation. If splitting occurs, pick the affected peppers right away. We see salsa in your future![7] —SN

Will sweet (bell) peppers continue to ripen and change colour after picking?

Bell peppers change colour as they mature—they generally end up red, orange, yellow, or purple, depending on the variety that is planted. The timing of the harvest will determine whether or not they change colour after picking. If the peppers are completely green when you harvest them, it's unlikely that they will undergo any further change. If they are already changing colour, there is a chance they may continue to do so after harvesting. There are no guarantees, however, and there is a further catch: They don't tend to ripen further in the refrigerator, and as fresh peppers don't store well for long periods without being in the fridge, you may wish to just use

Peppers change colour as they ripen on the plant.

them up, instead of waiting for the colour change to happen. If possible, we recommend allowing them to ripen on the plant.

And what about that colour change, anyway? How does it occur? As the seed matures inside the pepper fruit, the fruit undergoes several chemical changes, which influences pigmentation, sweetness, and even aroma. The chlorophyll that gives green peppers their colour breaks down and is replaced by other compounds, such as lutein and beta carotene. Due to all of these changes, ripened bell peppers are usually considered to have a superior sweet flavour compared to green ones.

Chili peppers also undergo a similar chemical (and colour) change.[8]—SN

Potatoes

8

Does a potato plant have to flower to produce potatoes?

Not all potato varieties will flower. (Some will do so only occasionally.) A lack of flowers will not affect tuber production, so there's no need to worry.

Many gardeners use the old adage to wait about three weeks after the potatoes have flowered to harvest, which is problematic if the plants don't flower. The easiest thing to do is excavate a small area of soil about four inches (ten centimetres) from the base of one of the plants to see if there are any tubers there. (If there aren't any, dig a little bit closer to the plant's roots.) If the tubers are not the size you desire, let the plants continue to grow for a bit longer.[1] — SN

There is nothing wrong with your potato plants if you don't see these.

My potato plants are producing weird things that look like little green tomatoes. What are they and should I do something about them?

Some potatoes will flower and produce fruit. The fruit may surprise you—they may look like miniature green to dark blue tomatoes (which makes sense as the two plants are from the same family and are very closely related). The fruit is poisonous, so do not sample it.

While you can plant the seeds that the fruits contain and grow potatoes from them, you will not get potatoes that are true to the parent plant; plus, it takes much longer to obtain a harvest. It's much easier to grow potatoes from a cut tuber, known as a seed potato. (Note the difference between this term and "potato seed," which describes the potato fruit.)

There is no need to remove the tomato-like fruit unless the plants are producing a massive amount of them, in which case the extra fruit is likely taking away from tuber production, which is what we really want. You may also want to remove the fruit to prevent children or pets (or unknowing passersby) from thinking they are tomatoes and ingesting them.[2] —SN

What does it mean to "chit" potatoes? How and why do you do it?

"Chitting" means to presprout your potatoes before you plant them. I have no idea where the term comes from, unless it is a derivation of "cheating," because, in a sense, when you chit your potatoes, you are getting a head start on those who simply plant their seed potatoes without chitting them!

To presprout your potatoes, inspect your bag or box of seed potatoes. Ones that are large and with many "eyes" can be cut into smaller portions, as long as there is a minimum of two eyes to each piece. Leave them in a dry and cool location, and allow the pieces to form calluses on the cut sides over a twenty-four-hour period. Smaller ones can stay intact, and if you had problems with insects and pathogens affecting your potatoes last season, forgo this step as those slices are large wounds that can provide easy access to pests and diseases.

Then simply set your potatoes with the ends of the most "eyes" up in shallow boxes or trays, such as paper egg cartons.

Place the trays in a warm, dry, and dark location for up to four weeks. Soon you will see the "eyes" sprout. When the "eyes" are no longer than one to two inches (three to five centimetres), plant them into soil that has warmed up to between 45 and 50°F (7 to 10°C). On the prairies, the time to plant potatoes can vary widely from year to year, but a good bet is not to start chitting your potatoes until the end of April.

Even if spring is early, and the soil warms up faster, waiting to complete chitting will pay dividends as presprouted potatoes will settle in faster and get a head start in growing, especially in cooler and heavier soils. Yields are likely to be larger too using this practice.

A word to the wise: Invest in certified seed potatoes as they are certified to be disease-free and meet quality assurance standards. Substandard seed potatoes will take longer to sprout, have uneven growth, be more prone to pests, and have lesser yields on average, not to mention the potential of spreading disease. —JM

Hilling potatoes — is it necessary?
If so, how is it done?

*Increase your potato harvest
by hilling your plants.*

The practice of hilling your potato plants works to increase yields. If you hill organic material around their stems, you increase the amount of room the underground stems have to grow, which leads to the potential for increased productivity. The additional covering also prevents tubers from forming close to the surface of the soil and being exposed to sunlight and photosynthesizing, which causes tubers to turn green and form toxic alkaloids in the skin, making them bitter.

The simplest way to hill potatoes starts with planting seed potatoes in a trench about twelve inches (thirty centimetres) deep that has been well dug over and has additional organic material added. Place your potatoes at the bottom of the trench and cover with soil. Once they are well established, about six inches (fifteen centimetres) high, fill in the trench so that just the top leaves are exposed. As the potato plants get bigger, keep repeating until they have grown out of the trench. At this point, you can continue to add soil around their stems or switch to a mulch, such as straw. Keep mounding soil or adding mulch around the plants until they start to flower, or until you run out of organic material, energy, or time.

Using a mulch for the last hilling works to keep weeds at bay, deters potato beetles, keeps the roots cooler, and conserves moisture in the soil.

The practice of growing potatoes in bags, mesh cylinders, and potato condos is based on the same technique of hilling, except you are using an above-ground container. The disadvantage of these containers is that the roots can either dry out due to evaporation around the sides or become too hot. After all, potatoes are meant to be a below-ground root vegetable. The benefits are all in the ease of harvesting as you simply tip over the container. No more putting your garden fork through the biggest potato!

A way to mitigate the downside of an above-ground container is to dig a hole the width of the container and sink the container into the hole at least partially, which serves to keep the roots cooler and yet keeps the convenience of harvesting.

One last word: Please do not use tires to grow potatoes. Some tires have many chemicals that can leach out into the soil and contaminate your potatoes. There are many much better options! —JM

What is the difference between determinate and indeterminate potatoes? How does selecting one type over another influence yield?

Trenching is an effective method of planting potatoes.

We are used to thinking of tomatoes as being indeterminate or determinate but not potatoes! But, in many ways, it is a matter of terminology. Usually potatoes are described as being a short-, mid-, or long-season crop, which roughly defines the length of time to maturity for many of the different varieties. However, those divisions do not provide gardeners with necessary information as to planting depth; requirement to hill; yield; and whether a variety is best grown in a container, tower, or bed.

Generally, plants are described as being determinate or indeterminate, if they produce flowers, fruit, and seeds. Examples are fruits (including citrus, berries, and stone fruits), peppers, beans, peas, and cucumbers. Those that are grown for their roots and leaves are not categorized in this way. A determinate variety is one that will grow to the size it will be, then flower and set fruit all at once. Once its fruit has matured, the plant will not produce more, no matter how much we want it to. It will not respond to methods we might use to coax further harvests. An indeterminate variety is one that will continue to grow in size, even while it is producing edibles.

Determinate potatoes are most often early- to mid-season varieties for they have the shortest time to maturity. The plants will grow to their mature size, then set tubers in a single layer. Determinate potato plants should be planted at a depth of four inches (ten centimetres). There is no need to hill determinate potato plants as this technique will not result in more tubers being produced. Simply mulch the plants to ensure that the developing tubers are not exposed to sunlight. Benefits to planting determinate potatoes include: their compact size is ideal for containers or small gardens; you can time a harvest to avoid potential damage by climate and pests; and you have the ability to plant another crop after the potatoes have been harvested. The downsides to determinate potatoes include: the harvest comes all at once; and some gardeners feel that these potatoes have less flavour. Notable determinate varieties include yellow-fleshed 'Yukon Gold', red-skinned 'Norland', and 'Chieftain'.

Indeterminate potatoes are "main crop" varieties that require over one hundred days to mature. These are the types of potatoes that should be hilled. Benefits to growing indeterminate potatoes include: a greater yield as tubers will grow in the soil at multiple levels; there will be a staggered harvest since you can remove new potatoes from the sides of the mounds while the plants continue to set tubers; and these varieties tend to work best for grow bags and potato towers. The disadvantages include: more work and caring for the plants over a longer period of time; greater potential for pests to find your crop or for pathogens to take hold; and, of course, the potential for early first frosts or other extreme weather may affect the plants. Good examples of indeterminate varieties include: 'Russet Burbank', 'Bintje', 'German Butterball', and 'Nicola'.

Weigh the advantages and disadvantages of both types of potatoes, and maximize your harvest by growing both![3] —JM

Squash, Pumpkins, and Cucumbers

9

Can I grow cucumbers, summer and winter squash, and pumpkins vertically?

Absolutely! There are several benefits to growing squash in this way, besides saving space. There is a reduced risk of soilborne diseases spreading through irrigation and splashing onto leaves and stems. Air circulation is usually improved with a trellised plant, which can be a huge boon when it comes to preventing problems such as powdery mildew. When left to grow horizontally, fruit will occasionally rot or soften where it touches the ground, which is not an issue with vertical growing.

Bear in mind that growing vertically is more difficult (and not really encouraged) for extremely long vines and gigantic fruit. You're not going to grow a prize-winning monster pumpkin on a trellis. The best types of squash to grow vertically tend to be varieties with short vines and small fruit. Squash that do not produce vines (for example, bush or container types) are not highly suitable for vertical growing either, although many of them may benefit from cages or other types of support.

A little creativity and an understanding of the incredible weight of even small squashes and pumpkin plants are needed when deciding what types of supports to use. Options include mounting a sturdy trellis to a fence or a wall, or using a securely anchored arbour or pergola. No matter what type of structure you choose, it must be heavy duty and solidly moored into the ground.

The other thing to consider is that squash and pumpkin plants do not climb on their own—you will need to install wires or string and tie the vines into position. This is a summer-long task. The plant ties must be soft and not too tightly secured to minimize stem injury and breakage. Some gardeners cut up cheap nylon stockings to use as ties; the stockings can also come in handy to use as "slings" to hold heavy fruit once it appears. (Pieces of old T-shirts work as well.)—SN

Squash can definitely go vertical!
Ensure your trellis is a strong one.

My cucumbers and squash had a lot of flowers this growing season, but they didn't produce very much fruit (or any at all!). Some of the fruit fell off the vines before they reached full size. What is going on here?

Partly formed fruit that drops off the vine or the utter absence of fruit is often caused by a pollination problem. Cucumbers, zucchini, and other squash sport separate male and female flowers on the same plant. Although some cucumbers and squash are parthenocarpic and do not need to be fertilized to set fruit, most species require a little assistance. With the help of pollinating insects, pollen from the male flowers is transferred to the female flowers, and then successful fertilization must occur for fruit to properly form. For this to work well, both the male and female flowers should be open at the same time. Some of the male flowers tend to open a bit earlier than the females, so occasionally the process does not take place as efficiently as it should.

A lack of pollinating insects (or not enough of them) in your veggie patch is another potential hurdle to properly formed fruit—or any fruit at all! If you are noticing a dearth of pollinating insects, plant a smorgasbord of tempting treats in and around your vegetables. Think of annual flowers such as calendula (*Calendula officinalis*), cosmos (*Cosmos bipinnatus*), borage (*Borago officinalis*), and nasturtiums (*Tropaeolum* spp.), or perennials such as smooth fleabane (*Erigeron glabellus*), asters (*Symphyotrichum* spp.), lupines (*Lupinus* spp.), or echinacea (*Echinacea purpurea*).

If you find poor pollination is a frequent occurrence with your squash and cucumber plants, you can always hand-pollinate the flowers. Look for the male and female flowers and identify which one is which. The females will have a tiny fruit growing beneath them; the males will be borne on stems. There will be far more male flowers than females; look for a nearly three-to-one ratio. Once you have the males picked out, carefully open the blossom and use a small artist's paintbrush or a cotton swab to collect as many pollen grains from the anther as possible. Move the brush to the female flower and transfer the pollen to the stigma. Don't forget that after you've taken the pollen from the male flowers, you can go ahead and harvest some of them—they are completely edible. Battered and fried squash blossoms, stuffed with tantalizing ingredients such as soft cheese, mushrooms, and bacon, are a treat to be savoured.

Weather (as usual) can play a role. Prolonged periods of drought or extreme rainfall can reduce the amount of pollen produced or cause other issues, which ultimately prevents the plants from focusing on creating fruit.[1]—SN

Pollination can sometimes be an issue for squash plants.

How can I keep pumpkins (or other large squash) from rotting on the ground while they grow and ripen?

There is nothing worse than going to harvest a pumpkin at the end of the growing season, only to find that it is soft and squishy where it has been touching the soil surface.

Fortunately, keeping the heavy fruits elevated is a quick fix—and you don't have to buy anything to do this. If you have a piece of scrap wood in your shed or garage, carefully slide it underneath the fruit. Gardeners press into service all kinds of creative recyclables for pumpkin stands: overturned plant pots or plastic storage totes, wooden crates or barrels, flattened cardboard boxes, and unused plant trays. If you are growing a pumpkin cultivar with small fruit, it may be useful to trellis the plants, to get both the vines and the fruit up off the ground. —SN

Seriously bitter cucumbers: How can I prevent this?

First, a bit of science: The compound that makes some cucumbers bitter is called, appropriately, cucurbitacin. Most of the time, the fruit doesn't contain a generous dose of cucurbitacin—it is usually confined to the other parts of the plant. But every so often, you get an unpleasant surprise when biting into a juicy cuke.

Unfortunately, you're not going to completely eliminate the possibility, but to reduce the chance of growing bitter cucumbers, try watering consistently. Dry cucumber plants may produce bitter fruit. (Strike a balance, however—do not overwater or you'll end up with other problems.) Plants that are grown in cool weather often sport bitter fruit: Keep your cucumbers cozy!

If you're worried about dining on bitter cucumbers, try peeling them first—it might improve the flavour.[2]—SN

Warm temperatures and sufficient water are the keys to a yummy cuke.

I'm really late with planting my garden. Are there any vegetable seeds I can plant in July that will give me a good harvest?

Yes, but it's important to remember that most of the crops we are listing are categorized as cool-season, which means they won't perform well (or even germinate with a huge rate of success) when the weather is hot and dry.

The other factor to consider is that after the third week of August the days are really shortening, and the energy of the sun is diminishing steadily, which will affect how quickly plants reach a harvesting size once they have germinated. Bear in mind as well that you may not be bringing all of these vegetables to full size—greens, for example, may be more on the "baby" side than fully mature.

Do not attempt to plant those vegetables that flower and are consumed either at the fruit stage or as seeds. Unless, of course, your goal is to grow them for their shoots and flowers, e.g., peas.

Choose edibles that are hardy or half-hardy and that can either tolerate light frost or convert starches to sugar once cooler nights are the norm, such as kale and others in the genus *Brassica*.

Obtain cultivars that have the shortest days to maturity, then calculate your time frame so that you will be able to harvest before your region's average first frost date in the autumn. (You can find out that information on the Environment Canada website: climate.weather.gc.ca.)

As you will be germinating seeds in the heat of the summer, it is of the utmost importance to ensure that there is constant soil moisture for effective germination and growth past the seedling stage when your edibles will be at their most vulnerable. Floating row covers laid over seeds and seedlings will help them to retain soil moisture and humidity, not to mention filter intense sunlight that will otherwise cause sunscald on tender leaves.

Once the nighttime temperatures are becoming cool, row covers will also serve to retain residual warmth around the plants, allowing them to continue growing even as temperatures dip.

Consider sowing these greens for the greatest chance of success:

* Arugula
* Beets—for their greens and possibly small roots
* Bok choi
* Carrots—short or mini varieties such as 'Little Fingers'
* Kale
* Leaf lettuce
* Mibuna
* Mizuna
* Peas—for shoots and flowers
* Radishes
* Spinach
* Swiss chard
* Tatsoi[3]

Kale may be sown late in the summer for an autumn harvest.

Harvesting and Storage

10

What is the best way to harvest leafy greens, such as lettuce and spinach, so that the crop lasts longer?

Many of your cool-season leafy greens can have an extended harvest over several weeks, or even the whole season, just by using a technique often called "cut and come again."

The technique involves commencing harvesting as soon as there are outer leaves that are young and around 2.5 to 4 inches (6 to 10 centimetres) long, with new leaves coming in at the centre growing point or from the rosette of the plant. Harvest the outer leaves by nipping them off at the base of the plant and leaving the new growth to take over. The golden rule is to always leave at least four new leaves, so that the plant can continue growing strongly. If too many leaves are removed at once, the plant weakens or growth stalls, as there isn't enough foliage left for efficient photosynthesizing to take place.

The benefits to cut-and-come-again are manifold. Continual removal of leaves prompts the plant to continue growing foliage rather than bolting by prematurely sending up a flowering stalk and setting seed. Young leaves are more likely to be tasty, tender, and nutritious and less likely to be damaged by weather events or pests. By continually harvesting, you are always paying attention to your edibles, and thus you will be able to spot problems sooner rather than later!

Eventually, the plant is going to say enough is enough and will want to go to seed. At that point, do remove it, and perhaps tuck in some more seedlings to grow, rather than trying to keep the initial plant going to its last leaf!

Greens that are exceedingly generous with their leaves include: kale, Swiss chard, spinach, arugula, endive, and lettuce, plus Asian greens such as mizuna and bok choi. The salad herb sorrel can be harvested vigorously throughout the season for its delicious lemony leaves.

Traditional root crops can also yield some young leaves early in the season before being left alone to develop their roots. Beets and turnips fall into this category.

Many herbs such as basil, parsley, and cilantro benefit from extensive cut-and-come-again harvesting, too! —JM

Spinach is a popular cut-and-come-again crop.

I have to harvest my winter squash before it is ripe on the vine. How can I ripen it indoors? What about my green tomatoes?

Planting winter squash varieties on the prairies always seems to be a bit of a gamble, given our often early frosts. Ideally, winter squash at harvest time should have developed a hard rind, sound hollow when tapped, and have a mature colour.

Impending frost will certainly damage the fruits, though if only a couple of degrees of frost are expected, using a floating row cover may be sufficient protection, so that the squashes can stay on the vine and continue to ripen for a little longer.

If the frost expected is a deep one, and the forecast is for continuing cold temperatures, then squashes that have started to turn colour should be cut off the vines, leaving about two inches (five centimetres) of the stalks attached to each fruit. Wash the skins immediately, and dry with a soft cloth, being careful not to damage the immature skins. Place in a warm, dry, and sunny location, so that the fruit can finish turning colour. Turn periodically so that all sides of the fruit receive sunlight. Immature fruit are perfectly edible, but will not have the same taste as mature fruit, nor will they store for as long.

You can either eat these while green or ripen them off the vine.

When frost threatens, squash may need to be harvested early.

Tomatoes, on the other hand, will mature well when taken off the vines still green, as they produce a plant hormone called ethylene that regulates plant growth, including ripening. Green tomatoes should be washed, dried carefully, and placed in single layers in cardboard trays with space between each fruit. They need to be out of the sun but in a dry and warm location. A simple trick my mother taught me to speed up the ripening process is to place a ripe banana with the tomatoes, as it gives off lots of ethylene. Check regularly to make sure that none are rotting, rather than ripening. I find that the flavour of tomatoes ripened this way is not as complex as vine-ripened ones, nor do they store as well. Roasting them afterward improves their flavour tremendously! —JM

Curing garlic and onions before storing ensures that they will not quickly perish.

How do I cure onions and garlic for storage?

All onions and garlic are not created equal, with some varieties being best for fresh eating, as they do not store well at all or even cured will last only a couple of months. Examples would be the large sweet onions such as 'Ailsa Craig' or 'Walla Walla'. Good storage onions are those that are smaller and not as juicy, and that have more sulphur content. Softneck garlic will store longer than hardneck as a rule, but most hardneck garlic will last five to nine months, which we find is more than long enough!

Once both onions and garlic have been harvested, inspect them quickly for defects, and set aside those for immediate consumption. It is not necessary to cut back the stems or roots, nor to clean off all soil clinging to them, as excessive cleaning may injure their soft and easily damaged skins at this point. Both are best laid out in a single layer on a drying rack or hung up in small bunches in a warm (59 to 77°F/15 to 25°C), dry, airy location, preferably out of direct sunlight, for at least two weeks.[1] During this time, the necks of the bulbs will shrink, cutting off nutrition from the dying leaves and sealing the flesh within. The basal plates will harden, signalling that the bulbs are going into dormancy, and the outer leaves will dry to a papery consistency.

Once the bulbs have finished curing, you can clip the remaining top leaves, cut the roots to about 3/4 inches (2 centimetres), and softly brush away any remaining soil. Inspect them to ensure that all bulbs are looking healthy.

Store in a cool, low-humidity environment away from light, such as a dry basement, either from the rafters or in storage racks, and check regularly to ensure that none are rotting.—JM

We wish you much success with
your prairie vegetable garden!

Acknowledgements

Janet and Sheryl would like to thank:

The incredible publishing team at TouchWood Editions: Taryn Boyd (publisher), Kate Kennedy (editorial coordinator), Paula Marchese (copy editor), Tori Elliott (marketing and publicity coordinator), Tree Abraham (designer), Meg Yamamoto (proofreader), and Pat Touchie (owner). We'd like to give a shout-out as well to Renée Layberry, who worked with us in the early stages of the manuscript. We are so appreciative of all of the hard work, dedication, and support from each and every one of you, and we are thrilled that our book is a part of the TouchWood Editions catalogue!

We'd also like to thank Kath Smyth, for her wealth of horticultural knowledge.

Janet is profoundly grateful to:

My co-author, Sheryl, for first approaching me with the idea that we could write a book together and then being such a fantastic and supportive writing partner!

My grandmother and mother for being such great gardeners themselves and assuming that of course I would follow in their footsteps. I think of both of them every day when I am in a garden!

My husband, Steve, my daughter, Jennifer, and, my son, David, for all the encouragement and support for my endeavours. Plus, their endless patience with me when my head is writing even when I am supposed to be paying attention to them!

All my friends who listen to me talk gardening year in and out and those special gardening friends who get down and dirty with me in gardening!

Sheryl sends out an immense amount of gratitude to:

My co-author, Janet—it's been such a blast going on this journey with you! I am delighted for the wonderful opportunity to work together!

My husband, Rob, my mum and dad, my brother Derek, and the rest of my family and friends, all of whom have offered unending encouragement of my writing and gardening pursuits. I can't thank you enough!

Notes

Introduction

1. University of California Cooperative Extension, "What Is the Difference Between a Fruit and a Vegetable?"

Chapter One

1. Boeckmann, "When to Water Your Vegetable Garden/Watering Chart," *The Old Farmer's Almanac*; Oder, "Are You Watering Your Veggies the Right Way?," Mother Nature Network (website); Vanheems, "Watering Your Vegetable Garden: How to Water Plants for Healthier Growth," GrowVeg (website).

2. Krans, "Plan Now for Crop Rotation in Your Vegetable Garden," Michigan State University Extension; Bradbury, "Crop Rotation for Growing Vegetables," GrowVeg (website); Kalynchuk, "Grow Your Own Food: A Guide to Crop Rotation for Your Vegetable Garden," Food Bloggers of Canada; Agriculture Classroom Canada, "Crop Rotation"; Pleasant, "Maintain Healthy Soil with Crop Rotation," *Mother Earth News*; Deep Green Permaculture, "Crop Rotation Systems for Annual Vegetables"; Waldin, *Biodynamic Gardening*, 144–149.

3. Macdonald, "Succession Planting," West Coast Seeds (website); Rude, "Calgary Horticultural Society: Succession Planting Guarantees Fresh Vegetables All Summer," *Calgary Herald*; York, "Tips for Growing Vegetable Gardens for Beginners, Experts and Everyone in Between," *Canadian Living*; Vanheems, "Succession Planting: Get More from Your Plot," GrowVeg (website); Iannotti, "How to Use Succession Planting in Your Garden," The Spruce (website); Hemenway, *Gaia's Garden*, 22–27; Jabbour, *The Year-Round Vegetable Gardener*, 14–27.

4. Heilig, "Select the Right Vegetable Garden Mulch," Michigan State University Extension; Relf, "Mulches for the Home Vegetable Garden," Virginia Cooperative Extension.

5. Parker, Miles, and Murray, "How to Install a Floating Row Cover," Washington State University; Gardener's Supply Company, "Using Garden Fabric (Row Covers)."

6. Jabbour, "6 High-Yield Vegetables," Savvy Gardening (website).

Chapter Two

1. Macdonald, "Bolting," West Coast Seeds (website); Vanheems, "How to Prevent Bolting in Vegetable Crops," GrowVeg (website).

2. University of Maryland Extension, "Edema—Vegetables."

3. Missouri Botanical Garden, "Oedema."

4. Grant, Amy, "Catfacing Fruit Deformity: Learn about Catfacing on Tomatoes," Gardening Know How (website); Carroll, "What Are Lygus Bugs: Tips for Lygus Bug Insecticide Control," Gardening Know How (website); University of California Cooperative Extension, "Tomato Catface/Cracking"; Gavloski, "Lygus Bugs in Field Crops," Government of Manitoba.

5. University of Manitoba, "Hail Damage."

6. Snyder and de Melo-Abreu, *Frost Protection: Fundamentals, Practice, and Economics*, vol. 1, Food and Agriculture Organization of the United Nations.

7. University of Maryland Extension, "Herbicide Damage—Vegetables"; Weller, "Understanding Herbicide Injury in Vegetable Crops and Labels," Purdue University; Van Dyk, "Herbicide Injury Symptoms in Tomatoes," ONVegetables (website); Grant, Bonnie L., "Herbicide Plant Damage: How to Treat Plants Accidentally Sprayed with Herbicide," Gardening Know How (website).

8. The Pennsylvania State University Extension, "Cool-Season vs. Warm-Season Vegetables"; The Pennsylvania State University Extension, "Seasonal Classification of Vegetables."

9. Spencer, "Growing Different Vegetable Crops: Introductory Vegetable Production," Government of Alberta; Lindgren and Browning, "Vegetable Garden Seed Storage and Germination Requirements," University of Nebraska Lincoln Extension.

Chapter Three

1. Boundary Garlic Farm (website), "Organic Seed Garlic."

2. VanDerZanden, "What Are Short Day and Long Day Plants?," Oregon State University Extension Service.

3. Ingham, "Soil Biology: The Food Web and Soil Health," Oregon State University.

4. Soil Health (website), "Fungi vs. Bacteria."

5. Jauron and Wallace, "Harvest, Dry and Store Onions, Garlic and Shallots," Iowa State University Extension and Outreach Yard and Garden.

6. Stanek, "Chefs Are Going Crazy for Black Garlic (and You Will, Too)," *Bon Appetit*.

Chapter Four

1. Alberta Government Agri-Facts, "Soil Temperature for Germination."

2. Grant, Amy, "Broccoli Not Forming Heads: Reasons Why My Broccoli Has No Head," Gardening Know How (website); *The Old Farmer's Almanac*, "Growing Broccoli: Planting, Growing, and Harvesting Broccoli."

3. University of Illinois Extension, "Watch Your Garden Grow: Cabbage."

4. University of Minnesota Extension, "Growing Kohlrabi in Home Gardens."

5. Anything Grows (website), "Vegetable Seed Start Dates."

6. University of New Hampshire Cooperative Extension, "Brussels Sprouts Variety Trial and Topping Study, 2013 and 2014."

Chapter Five

1. University of Massachusetts Extension, "Northern Root Knot Nematodes in Vegetable Crops"; Government of Alberta, "Diseases of Vegetables—Carrots"; University of Illinois Extension, "Carrots."

2. Cornell University, "Celery"; Utah State University Extension, "Celery."

3. Kansas State University Research and Extension, "Intensive Spacing for Raised Beds"; Pavlis, "Why Do Beets Always Need to Be Thinned?," Garden Fundamentals (website); Perry, "Growing Your Own Beets," University of Vermont.

4. Trail, "What Is Wrong with My Lettuce?"

5. Agriculture Victoria, "Tipburn in Lettuce"; University of Maryland Extension, "Lettuce."

Chapter Six

1. University of Illinois Extension, "Peas"; Albert, "Pea Growing Problems: Troubleshooting," Harvest to Table (website).

2. Albert, "Bean Growing Problems: Troubleshooting," Harvest to Table (website).

3. Macdonald, "Growing Food in Part Shade," West Coast Seeds (website); Tilley, "Vegetables That Grow in Shade: How to Grow Vegetables in Shade," Gardening Know How (website); Jabbour, "Vegetables for Shade: Niki's Top Picks!," Savvy Gardening (website).

4. Ohio State University, "7 Causes for Corn Emergence Problems," Farm Progress (website); Nielson, "When Good Corn Fields Turn Bad," Purdue University; Johnson, "Reduced Ear Problem in Sweet Corn," University of Delaware; Butts-Wilmsmeyer, Seebauer, Singleton, and Below, "Weather During Key Growth Stages Explains Grain Quality and Yield of Maize," *Agronomy*; University of Saskatchewan, "Corn."

5. MacKenzie, "Growing Sweet Corn in Home Gardens," University of Minnesota Extension; Iowa State University Extension and Outreach, "What Are the Differences Between the Various Types of Sweet Corn?"

Chapter Seven

1. University of Saskatchewan, "Blossom Drop in Tomatoes Reduces Yield."

2. Hole and Fallis, *Lois Hole's Tomato Favorites*, 10–11.

3. LeHoullier, *Epic Tomatoes*, 92, 94–95.

4. LeHoullier, *Epic Tomatoes*, 94–95.

5. Gardener's Supply Company (website), "How to Control Blossom-End Rot of Tomato"; University of Illinois Extension, "Integrated Pest Management: Blossom-End Rot of Tomato"; Grant, Bonnie L., "Using Eggs as Raw Fertilizer: Tips for Fertilizing with Raw Eggs," Gardening Know How (website); University of Saskatchewan, "Blossom End Rot Reduces Yield."

6. Grant, Bonnie L.,"Tips to Stop Sunscald on Pepper Plants," Gardening Know How (website).

7. Grant, Amy, "Jalapeño Skin Cracking: What Is Corking on Jalapeño Peppers," Gardening Know How (website).

8. Compound Interest (website), "The Chemistry of Bell Peppers—Colour and Aroma"; Pleasant, "Do All Peppers Start Out Green?," *Mother Earth News*; NatureFresh Farms (website), "Why Are Bell Peppers Different Colors?"

Chapter Eight

1. Hodgson, "Why Don't Some Potato Plants Bloom? My Potato Plants Aren't Blooming!," Laidback Gardener (website).

2. Voyle, "What Fruit Is Growing on My Potato Plants?," Michigan State University.

3. Ellis, "What Are the Differences between Determinate and Indeterminate Potatoes?," Gardening Know How (website); How to Grow Potatoes (website), "Indeterminate Seed Potatoes"; Seed Potatoes (website), "Potato Varieties"; Seasonal Ontario Food (website), "Determinate and Indeterminate Vegetables."

Chapter Nine

1. Jabbour, "Pollinating Squash, Cucumbers and Pumpkins," Savvy Gardening (website); Anson, "Cucumber, Squash and Pumpkin (Cucurbits) Problems," Missouri Botanical Garden; Glen, "Why Are My Squash Rotting?," North Carolina Cooperative Extension; Gilmer, "Gardeners, Eat Your Squash Blossoms," *Seattle Times*.

2. Myers, "Cucumber Bitterness Explained," Oregon State University, OSU Extension Service.

3. Vanderlinden, "Vegetables and Herbs to Plant in July," The Spruce (website); Jacobs, "Attention Gardeners! Perfect Vegetables for Planting in July!," CBC; MacKenzie, "Planting Vegetables in Midsummer for Fall Harvest," University of Minnesota Extension.

Chapter Ten

1. Pleasant, "Curing Onions for Storage," GrowVeg (website).

Sources

Agriculture Classroom Canada. "Crop Rotation." Accessed June 7, 2019. https:// aitc-canada.ca/en-ca/learn-about-agriculture/category/farming-the-environment/crop -rotation.

Agriculture Victoria. "Tipburn in Lettuce." Accessed June 7, 2019. agriculture.vic.gov .au/agriculture/pests-diseases-and-weeds/plant-diseases/vegetable/tipburn-in-lettuce.

Albert, Steve. "Bean Growing Problems: Troubleshooting." Harvest to Table (website). Accessed June 8, 2019. harvesttotable.com/bean_growing_problems_troubles/.

————. "Pea Growing Problems: Troubleshooting." Harvest to Table (website). Accessed June 8, 2019. harvesttotable.com/pea_growing_problems_troublesh/.

Alberta Government Agri-Facts. "Soil Temperature for Germination." Accessed June 7, 2019. open.alberta.ca/publications/2415866.

Anson, Ronda. "Cucumber, Squash and Pumpkin (Cucurbits) Problems." Missouri Botanical Garden. Accessed June 10, 2019. missouribotanicalgarden.org/gardens -gardening/your-garden/help-for-the-home-gardener/advice-tips-resources/visual-guides /cucumber-squash-pumpkin-cucurbits-problems.aspx.

Anything Grows (website). "Vegetable Seed Start Dates." Accessed June 7, 2019. anythinggrowsalberta.com/plants/seeds/seed-starting-guides/vegetable-seed-start-dates/.

Boeckmann, Catherine. "When to Water Your Vegetable Garden/Watering Chart." *The Old Farmer's Almanac*, May 29, 2019. almanac.com/content/when-water-your -vegetable-garden-watering-chart.

Boundary Garlic Farm (website). "Organic Seed Garlic." Accessed June 7, 2019. garlicfarm.ca/.

Bradbury, Kate. "Crop Rotation for Growing Vegetables." GrowVeg (website). November 12, 2010. growveg.com/guides/crop-rotation-for-growing-vegetables/.

Butts-Wilmsmeyer, Carrie J., Juliann R. Seebauer, Lee Singleton, and Frederick E. Below. "Weather During Key Growth Stages Explains Grain Quality and Yield of Maize." *Agronomy*, January 2, 2019. https://www.mdpi.com/2073-4395/9/1/16.

Carroll, Jackie. "What Are Lygus Bugs: Tips for Lygus Bug Insecticide Control." Gardening Know How (website). April 5, 2018. gardeningknowhow.com/plant -problems/pests/insects/lygus-bug-control.htm.

Compound Interest (website). "The Chemistry of Bell Peppers—Colour and Aroma." July 5, 2016. compoundchem.com/2016/07/05/bell-peppers/.

Cornell University. "Celery." 2006. Accessed June 11, 2019. gardening.cornell.edu /homegardening/sceneb528.html.

Deep Green Permaculture. "Crop Rotation Systems for Annual Vegetables." Accessed June 7, 2019. deepgreenpermaculture.com/articles-and-reference-material/crop -rotation-systems-for-annual-vegetables/.

Ellis, Mary Ellen. "What Are the Differences between Determinate and Indeterminate Potatoes?" Gardening Know How (website). April 3, 2018. gardeningknowhow.com /edible/vegetables/potato/determinate-indeterminate-potatoes.htm.

Gardener's Supply Company (website). "How to Control Blossom-End Rot on Tomatoes." March 14, 2019. gardeners.com/how-to/blossom-end-rot/5354.html.

————. "Using Garden Fabric (Row Covers)." February 26, 2019. gardeners.com /how-to/row-covers/5111.html.

Gavloski, John. "Lygus Bugs in Field Crops." Government of Manitoba. February 2019. gov.mb.ca/agriculture/crops/insects/print,lygus-bug.html.

Gilmer, Maureen. "Gardeners, Eat Your Squash Blossoms." *Seattle Times*, July 11, 2009. seattletimes.com/life/lifestyle/gardeners-eat-your-squash-blossoms/.

Glen, Charlotte. "Why Are My Squash Rotting?" North Carolina Cooperative Extension. October 31, 2013. pender.ces.ncsu.edu/2013/05/why-are-my-squash-rotting/.

Government of Alberta. "Diseases of Vegetables – Carrots." Accessed June 7, 2019. alberta.ca/diseases-of-vegetables-carrots.aspx#toc-13.

Grant, Amy. "Broccoli Not Forming Heads: Reasons Why My Broccoli Has No Head." Gardening Know How (website). April 4, 2018. gardeningknowhow.com/edible /vegetables/broccoli/broccoli-not-forming-heads.htm.

————. "Catfacing Fruit Deformity: Learn about Catfacing on Tomatoes." Gardening Know How (website). April 4, 2018. gardeningknowhow.com/edible/vegetables/tomato /catfacing-fruit-deformity.htm.

————. "Jalapeño Skin Cracking: What Is Corking on Jalapeño Peppers." Gardening Know How (website). April 4, 2018. gardeningknowhow.com/edible/vegetables/pepper /jalapeno-skin-cracking.htm.

Grant, Bonnie L. "Herbicide Plant Damage: How to Treat Plants Accidentally Sprayed with Herbicide." Gardening Know How (website). April 5, 2018. gardeningknowhow .com/plant-problems/environmental/herbicide-plant-damage.htm.

————. "Tips to Stop Sunscald on Pepper Plants." Gardening Know How (website). April 5, 2018. gardeningknowhow.com/edible/vegetables/pepper/pepper-sunscald.htm.

————. "Using Eggs as Raw Fertilizer: Tips for Fertilizing with Raw Eggs." Gardening Know How (website). April 4, 2018. gardeningknowhow.com/garden-how-to/soil -fertilizers/fertilizing-with-raw-eggs.htm.

Heilig, Gray. "Select the Right Vegetable Garden Mulch." Michigan State University Extension. May 30, 2012. canr.msu.edu/news/select_the_right_vegetable_garden _mulch.

Hemenway, Toby. *Gaia's Garden*. Vermont: Chelsea Green Publishing, 2009.

Hodgson, Larry. "Why Don't Some Potato Plants Bloom? My Potato Plants Aren't Blooming!" Laidback Gardener (website). August 4, 2016. laidbackgardener.blog/tag /why-dont-some-potato-plants-bloom/.

Hole, Lois, and Jill Fallis. *Lois Hole's Tomato Favorites*. Edmonton: Lone Pine Publishing, 1996.

How to Grow Potatoes (website). "Indeterminate Seed Potatoes." Accessed June 9, 2019. howtogrowpotatoes.website/index.php/seed-potatoes-planting-sprouting-chitting-storing/indeterminate-seed-potatoes/.

Iannotti, Marie. "How to Use Succession Planting in Your Garden." The Spruce (website). June 1, 2019. thespruce.com/succession-planting-1403366.

Ingham, Elaine R. "Soil Biology: The Food Web and Soil Health." Oregon State University. Accessed June 7, 2019. web.extension.illinois.edu/soil/SoilBiology/fw&soilhealth.htm.

Iowa State University Extension and Outreach. "What Are the Differences Between the Various Types of Sweet Corn?" Accessed June 9, 2019. hortnews.extension.iastate.edu/faq/what-are-differences-between-various-types-sweet-corn.

Jabbour, Niki. "Pollinating Squash, Cucumbers and Pumpkins." Savvy Gardening (website). Accessed June 10, 2018. savvygardening.com/pollinating-squash-cucumbers-pumpkins/.

———. "6 High-Yield Vegetables." Savvy Gardening (website). Accessed June 7, 2019. savvygardening.com/6-high-yield-vegetables/.

———. "Vegetables for Shade: Niki's Top Picks!" Savvy Gardening (website). Accessed June 8, 2019. savvygardening.com/nikis-top-5-vegetables-for-shade/.

———. The Year-Round Vegetable Gardener. North Adams, Massachusetts: Storey Publishing, 2011.

Jacobs, Hanna. "Attention Gardeners! Perfect Vegetables for Planting in July!" CBC. June 29, 2015. cbc.ca/stevenandchris/food/planting-in-july.

Jauron, Richard, and Greg Wallace. "Harvest, Dry and Store Onions, Garlic and Shallots." Iowa State University Extension and Outreach Yard and Garden. Accessed April 5, 2019. extension.iastate.edu/news/yard-and-garden-harvest-dry-store-onions-garlic-shallots.

Johnson, Gordon. "Reduced Ear Problem in Sweet Corn." University of Delaware. August 1, 2013. extension.udel.edu/weeklycropupdate/?p=6114.

Kalynchuk, Redawna. "Grow Your Own Food: A Guide to Crop Rotation for Your Vegetable Garden." Food Bloggers of Canada (website). Accessed June 7, 2019. foodbloggersofcanada.com/a-guide-to-crop-rotation-for-your-vegetable-garden/.

Kansas State University Research and Extension. "Intensive Spacing for Raised Beds." Accessed June 8, 2019. johnson.k-state.edu/docs/lawn-and-garden/in-house-publications/vegetables/Intensive%20Spacing%20for%20Raised%20Beds_13.pdf.

Krans, Rebecca. "Plan Now for Crop Rotation in Your Vegetable Garden." Michigan State University Extension. April 3, 2014. canr.msu.edu/news/plan_now_for_crop_rotation_in_your_vegetable_garden.

LeHoullier, Craig. Epic Tomatoes: How to Select and Grow the Best Varieties of All Time. North Adams: Storey Publishing, 2014.

Lindgren, Dale T., and Sarah J. Browning. "Vegetable Garden Seed Storage and Germination Requirements." University of Nebraska Lincoln Extension. June 2014. extensionpublications.unl.edu/assets/pdf/g2090.pdf.

Macdonald, Mark. "Bolting." West Coast Seeds (website). June 5, 2018. westcoastseeds
.com/blogs/garden-wisdom/bolting.

——. "Growing Food in Part Shade." West Coast Seeds (website). February 11,
2019. westcoastseeds.com/blogs/garden-wisdom/growing-food-in-part-shade?gclid=EAIa
IQobChMIzsjioYCf4gIVFcZkCh0wqgEeEAAYASAAEgJo1PD_BwE.

——. "Succession Planting." West Coast Seeds (website). April 22, 2017.
westcoastseeds.com/blogs/garden-wisdom/stagger-sowing-for-a-longer-harvest.

MacKenzie, Jill. "Growing Sweet Corn in Home Gardens." University of Minnesota
Extension. 2018. extension.umn.edu/vegetables/growing-sweet-corn.

——. "Planting Vegetables in Midsummer for Fall Harvest." University of
Minnesota Extension. 2018. extension.umn.edu/planting-and-growing-guides/planting-
vegetables-midsummer-fall-harvest.

Missouri Botanical Garden. "Oedema." Accessed June 7, 2019.
missouribotanicalgarden.org/gardens-gardening/your-garden/help-for-the-home
-gardener/advice-tips-resources/pests-and-problems/environmental/oedema.aspx.

Myers, Jim. "Cucumber Bitterness Explained." Oregon State University, OSU
Extension Service. Accessed April 1, 2019. extension.oregonstate.edu/news/cucumber
-bitterness-explained.

NatureFresh Farms (website). "Why Are Bell Peppers Different Colors?" April 25, 2018.
naturefresh.ca/bell-pepper-faqs-facts/.

Nielson, R.L. (Bob). "When Good Corn Fields Turn Bad." Purdue University. 2001.
agry.purdue.edu/ext/corn/news/articles.01/Uneven_Stands-0530.html.

Oder, Tom. "Are You Watering Your Veggies the Right Way?" Mother Nature Network
(website). August 19, 2016. mnn.com/your-home/organic-farming-gardening/stories/are
-you-watering-your-veggies-right-way.

Ohio State University. "7 Causes for Corn Emergence Problems." Farm Progress.
Accessed June 9, 2019. farmprogress.com/corn/7-causes-corn-emergence-problems.

The Old Farmer's Almanac. "Growing Broccoli: Planting, Growing, and Harvesting
Broccoli." Accessed June 7, 2019. almanac.com/plant/broccoli#.

O'Meara, Carol. "Garden Produce and Flooded Fields." Colorado State University
Extension. Accessed June 7, 2019. http://csuhort.blogspot.com/2013/09/garden
-produce-and-flooded-fields.html.

Parker, Joyce, Carol Miles, and Todd Murray. "How to Install a Floating Row Cover."
Washington State University. 2012. cru.cahe.wsu.edu/CEPublications/FS089E
/FS089E.pdf.

Pavlis, Robert. "Why Do Beets Always Need to Be Thinned?" Garden Fundamentals
(website). Accessed June 8, 2019. gardenfundamentals.com/why-beets-need-thinning/.

The Pennsylvania State University Extension. "Cool-Season vs. Warm-Season
Vegetables." April 26, 2017. https://extension.psu.edu/cool-season-vs-warm-season
-vegetables.

————. "Seasonal Classification of Vegetables." October 22, 2007. https://extension .psu.edu/seasonal-classification-of-vegetables.

Perry, Dr. Leonard. "Growing Your Own Beets." University of Vermont. Accessed June 8, 2019. pss.uvm.edu/ppp/articles/beets.html.

Pleasant, Barbara. "Curing Onions for Storage." GrowVeg (website). July 19, 2013. growveg.com/guides/curing-onions-for-storage/.

————. "Do All Peppers Start Out Green?" *Mother Earth News*, July 30, 2008. motherearthnews.com/organic-gardening/peppers-start-out-green-zb0z08zblon.

————. "Maintain Healthy Soil with Crop Rotation." *Mother Earth News*, February /March 2010. motherearthnews.com/organic-gardening/gardening-techniques/healthy -soil-crop-rotation-zmaz10fmzraw.

Relf, Diane. "Mulches for the Home Vegetable Garden." Virginia Cooperative Extension. 2015. pubs.ext.vt.edu/content/dam/pubs_ext_vt_edu/426/426-326/426 -326_pdf.pdf.

Rude, Elaine. "Calgary Horticultural Society: Succession Planting Guarantees Fresh Vegetables All Summer." *Calgary Herald*, May 10, 2017. calgaryherald.com/life/food /calgary-horticultural-society-succession-planting-guarantees-fresh-veggies-all-summer.

Seasonal Ontario Food. "Determinate and Indeterminate Vegetables." November 2, 2012. seasonalontariofood.blogspot.com/2012/11/determinate-and-indeterminate -vegetables.html.

Seed Potatoes (website). "Potato Varieties." Accessed June 9, 2019. seedpotatoes.ca /potato-store/.

Snyder, Richard L., and J. Paulo de Melo-Abreu. *Frost Protection: Fundamentals, Practice, and Economics*. Vol. 1. Rome: Food and Agriculture Organization of the United Nations, 2005. fao.org/3/y7223e/y7223e00.htm#Contents.

Soil Health (website). "Fungi vs. Bacteria." Accessed June 7, 2019. soilhealth.com/soil -health/organisms/fungi-bact/.

Spencer, Rob. "Growing Different Vegetable Crops: Introductory Vegetable Production." Government of Alberta. February 24, 2014. agric.gov.ab.ca/crops/hort /bv2014/growing-dif-veg-crops-2014.pdf.

Stanek, Amiel. "Chefs Are Going Crazy for Black Garlic (and You Will, Too)." *Bon Appetit*, January 25, 2016. https://www.bonappetit.com/test-kitchen/how-to/article /black-garlic.

Tilley, Nikki. "Vegetables That Grow in Shade: How to Grow Vegetables in Shade." Gardening Know How (website). May 30, 2016. gardeningknowhow.com/edible /vegetables/vgen/shade-vegetables.htm.

Trail, Gayla. "What Is Wrong with My Lettuce?" Accessed August 19, 2019. https:// www.hgtv.com/outdoors/flowers-and-plants/vegetables/what-is-wrong-with-my-lettuce.

University of California Cooperative Extension. "Tomato Catface/Cracking." 2017. vric.ucdavis.edu/veg_info/catface.htm.

————. "What Is the Difference Between a Fruit and a Vegetable?" Accessed June 7, 2019. vric.ucdavis.edu/main/faqs.htm.

University of Illinois Extension. "Carrots." Accessed June 7, 2019. extension.illinois .edu/veggies/carrot.cfm.

————. "Integrated Pest Management: Blossom-End Rot of Tomato." 2002. ipm .illinois.edu/diseases/series900/rpd906/index.html.

————. "Peas." Accessed June 8, 2019. extension.illinois.edu/veggies/peas.cfm.

————. "Watch Your Garden Grow: Cabbage." Accessed April 2, 2019. web.extension .illinois.edu/veggies/cabbage.cfm.

University of Manitoba. "Hail Damage." Accessed June 7, 2019. umanitoba.ca/faculties /afs/hort_inquiries/845.html.

University of Maryland Extension. "Edema—Vegetables." Accessed June 7, 2019. extension.umd.edu/hgic/topics/edema-vegetables.

————. "Herbicide Damage—Vegetables." Accessed June 7, 2019. extension.umd.edu /hgic/topics/herbicide-damage-vegetables.

————. "Lettuce." Accessed June 7, 2019. extension.umd.edu/hgic/topics/lettuce.

University of Massachusetts Extension. "Northern Root Knot Nematodes in Vegetable Crops." Accessed June 7, 2019. ag.umass.edu/sites/ag.umass.edu/files/fact-sheets/pdf /nrkn_in_veg_crops_final-1.pdf.

University of Minnesota Extension. "Growing Kohlrabi in Home Gardens." Accessed April 2, 2019. extension.umn.edu/vegetables/growing-kohlrabi#watering-600810.

University of New Hampshire Cooperative Extension. "Brussels Sprouts Variety Trial and Topping Study, 2013 and 2014." Accessed June 7, 2019. extension.unh.edu /resource/research-report-brussels-sprouts-variety-trial-and-topping-study-2013-2014.

University of Saskatchewan. "Blossom Drop in Tomatoes Reduces Yield." February 7, 2018. gardening.usask.ca/articles-disorders/blossom-drop-in-tomatoes.php.

————. "Blossom End Rot Reduces Yield." February 2, 2018. gardening.usask.ca /articles-disorders/blossom-end-rot.php.

————. "Corn." Accessed June 9, 2019. usask.ca/agriculture/plantsci/vegetable /vegetable/vrecommendvar.htm#corn.

Utah State University Extension. "Celery." Accessed June 11, 2019. extension.usu.edu /yardandgarden/vegetables/celery.

Vanderlinden, Colleen. "Vegetables and Herbs to Plant in July." The Spruce (website). February 10, 2019. thespruce.com/planting-vegetables-and-herbs-in-july-2540000.

VanDerZanden, Ann Marie. "What Are Short Day and Long Day Plants?" Oregon State University Extension Service. Accessed June 7, 2019. extension.oregonstate.edu /news/what-are-short-day-long-day-plants.

Van Dyk, Dennis. "Herbicide Injury Symptoms in Tomatoes." ONVegetables (website). May 23, 2017. onvegetables.com/2017/05/23/herbicide-injury-symptoms-in-tomatoes/.

Vanheems, Benedict. "How to Prevent Bolting in Vegetable Crops." GrowVeg (website). June 30, 2016. growveg.com/guides/how-to-prevent-bolting-in-vegetable-crops/.

————. "Succession Planting: Get More from Your Plot." GrowVeg (website). July 24, 2015. growveg.com/guides/succession-planting-get-more-from-your-plot/.

————. "Watering Your Vegetable Garden: How to Water Plants for Healthier Growth." GrowVeg (website). June 19, 2015. growveg.com/guides/watering-your -vegetable-garden-how-to-water-plants-for-healthier-growth/.

Voyle, Gretchen. "What Fruit Is Growing on My Potato Plants?" Michigan State University. September 12, 2014. canr.msu.edu/news/what_are_those_fruit_growing _on_my_potato_plants.

Waldin, Monty. *Biodynamic Gardening.* London: DK Publishing, 2015.

Weller, Stephen. "Understanding Herbicide Injury in Vegetable Crops and Labels." Purdue University. Accessed June 7, 2019. ag.purdue.edu/hla/fruitveg/Presentations /Weller_UnderstandingHerbicide_IHC2017.pdf.

York, Karen. "Tips for Growing Vegetable Gardens for Beginners, Experts and Everyone in Between." *Canadian Living,* May 1, 2016. canadianliving.com/home-and -garden/gardening/article/tips-for-growing-a-vegetable-garden-for-beginners-experts-and -everyone-in-between.

Index

Page numbers in italics refer to photographs.

About the Authors

SHERYL NORMANDEAU was born and raised in the Peace Country region of northern Alberta and has made Calgary her home since 1994. A writer and master gardener, Sheryl holds a bachelor's degree in English, as well as a Prairie Horticulture Certificate and an Urban Sustainable Agriculture Certificate. Since 2013, she has served as the online Ask an Expert for the Calgary Horticultural Society. She works at the Calgary Public Library—besides gardening, books of all kinds are her grand passion! She is a small-space gardener (on a tiny balcony and in a plot in a nearby community garden) and she is most enthusiastic about growing veggies. She lives with her husband, Rob, their rescue cat, Smudge, and a tankful of freshwater fish. Find Sheryl at Flowery Prose (floweryprose.com), on Facebook (@FloweryProse), Twitter (@Flowery_Prose), and Instagram (flowery_prose).

JANET MELROSE was born in Trinidad, West Indies, and immigrated to Canada in 1964. She has lived in Calgary since 1969. She is a master gardener and the creator and owner of the successful horticulture business Calgary's Cottage Gardener, which specializes in garden education, horticultural therapy, and advocating for sustainable local food systems. She holds bachelor's degrees in sociology and history, a Prairie Horticulture Certificate, and a Horticultural Therapy Certificate. Janet is a lifelong gardener, coming from a heritage of English gardening. She has a large garden at home in the suburbs of Calgary that can only be described as a typical cottage garden. She cares for eight other gardens throughout Calgary through her work as a horticultural therapist, as well as a bed at the Inglewood Community Garden. She is married to Steve and has two children, Jennifer and David. Three cats, Patrick, Theo, and Mia, currently own their home and patrol against the deer, hares, squirrels, skunk, mice, and assorted birds that believe the garden is theirs, too! Connect with Janet on Facebook (@Calgarys-Cottage-Gardener), Twitter (@CalCottageGrdnr), and Instagram (CalgarysCottageGardener).

NOTES

NOTES

NOTES

About the Series

It looks like you've discovered the **Guides for the Prairie Gardener.** This budding series puts the combined knowledge of two lifelong prairie gardeners at your grubby fingertips. Whether you've just cleared a few square feet for your first bed of veggies or are a seasoned green thumb stumped by that one cultivar you can't seem to master, we think you'll find Janet and Sheryl the ideal teachers. Find answers on seeds, soil, trees, flowers, weather, climate, pests, pots, and quite a few more. These slim but mighty volumes, handsomely designed, make great companions at the height of summer in the garden trenches and during cold winter days planning the next season. With regional expertise, elegance, and a sense of humour, Janet and Sheryl take your questions and turn them into prairie gardening inspiration. For more information, and for other titles in the series, visit touchwoodeditions.com/guidesprairiegardener.